Nathan Haskell Dole

The Mistakes we Make

A practical manual of corrections in history, language, and fact, for readers and

writers

Nathan Haskell Dole

The Mistakes we Make
A practical manual of corrections in history, language, and fact, for readers and writers

ISBN/EAN: 9783337386016

Printed in Europe, USA, Canada, Australia, Japan

Cover: Foto ©Lupo / pixelio.de

More available books at **www.hansebooks.com**

The Mistakes We Make

A Practical Manual of Corrections

IN

HISTORY, LANGUAGE, AND FACT, FOR READERS
AND WRITERS

COMPILED AND EDITED

BY

NATHAN HASKELL DOLE

NEW YORK: 46 East 14th Street

THOMAS Y. CROWELL & COMPANY

BOSTON: 100 Purchase Street

EDITOR'S NOTE.

Solomon says, " Faithful are the wounds of a friend." This manual tries to take the place of a friend, good-natured and yet critical. The captious, carping criticism that finds fault in a selfish, egotistical, pharisaical, and condescending spirit does little good. Nor does it advantage a man to have his faults pointed out in the presence of others. This little book is the counsellor for the closet. We all make mistakes of every kind. The old pessimistic philosophy says the greatest mistake is living. But since we are here in this world it is our duty to improve ourselves, and when our faults are brought to our notice, to amend them. There is not one man, woman, or child in this wide country that does not occasionally perpetrate some of the blunders in fact, grammar, style, here held up to comment. Undoubtedly hundreds more might have been added to advantage. But the editor's scoop-net was not large enough, and it is to be doubted if a single book would hold them all. They have been gathered from all sources: the basis of the book is a little

English treatise bearing the same title and edited by C. E. Clarke.

But this material has been largely transposed and rewritten. "Notes and Queries," that *omnium gatherum* of facts and fancies, has been ransacked, and many other periodicals and books — notably Wilhelm Edel von Janko's "Fabeln und Geschichte" — have been put under contribution.

There is nothing original about the book or its contents. Such volumes have been made before. There is a French work in fifteen volumes, containing a vast quantity of historical mistakes rectified at great length. In the eleventh century the learned 'Ali ibn Muhammad ibn 'Othmar, called Al Hariri, or the Silken, wrote a book entitled "The Pearl," or "The Pearl of the Diver," in which he pointed out a multitude of errors commonly made by the educated people of his day. Very likely among the lost works of Solomon there was one of the same kind. Prophets have arisen from time to time throughout the ages.

It is to be hoped that no errors will be found in a book which aims to correct errors. Yet many may cry, "Physician, heal thyself." The editor can only say that he has endeavored to stick to accuracy, but if others discover slips that he has made he will be glad to have them pointed out.

NATHAN HASKELL DOLE.

BOSTON, Aug. 25, 1898.

CONTENTS

THE MISTAKES WE MAKE.

CHAPTER I.

THINGS CALLED BY WRONG NAMES.

TRADITION, carelessness, and ignorance are responsible for many instances of wrong names applied to well-known objects. The conservatism that contents itself with the " well enough " permits the error to be perpetuated, even though advance in knowledge may have shown the fallacy.

Bunker Hill Monument. — Thus we still celebrate the Battle of Bunker Hill, and the monument that dominates Charlestown is called Bunker Hill monument. The battle took place on Breed's Hill.

Cleopatra's Needle. — The so-called " Cleopatra's Needle " was not originally set up by Cleopatra, or in her honor. The Needle, which is now on the Thames embankment in London, was first erected by Thothmes, B.C. 1600, in front of the temple of the Sun-god at On or Heliopolis. When Rameses II., B.C. 1333, ruled the Nile Valley, he added his name to his predecessor's. Cleopatra had the monolith taken with others from its original position and reërected in Alexandria, in order to adorn her palace at Laodicea.

Pompey's Pillar. — "Pompey's Pillar" has no historical connection with that personage. According to the inscription it was erected by Publius, Prefect of Egypt, A.D. 926, in honor of the Emperor Diocletian. Professor Mahaffy claims that it was erected two centuries before Christ by one of the Ptolemies, and that, from being a four-sided obelisk, it was made round by order of the Emperor, and topped with a capital on which was placed his statue.

Job's Stone. — The belief in the existence of the "Stone of Job" must be given up. Near the village of Saijdeh, situated on the road leading from Damascus to Mizerebi, in a district which, according to tradition, was the birthplace of Job, is a hill known as the "Hill of Job." Near this hill is a stone on which the patriarch is said to have rested. This stone was, until recently, surrounded by a Moslem shrine which has fallen into decay, exposing the stone to view. It commemorates a visit of Rameses, the Pharaoh of the oppression. On the top of the stone is a tablet containing a representation of the winged disc of the sun, under which, in the usual Egyptian style, is the figure of the monarch giving offering to the Goddess Maat. Over the head of the king is his hieroglyphic name: "*Ra-user-ma-setep-en-Ra*" — "The Sun, powerful by truth, approved by the Sun," which was the throne name of Rameses II.

So the tomb of Abel fifteen miles north of Damascus derived its name from the ancient city of Abila and never held the body of the first man murdered.

The Egyptian Sphinx. — Strict accuracy would not permit the stone-hewed statue of the goddess Armachis in the Valley of the Nile to be called "the Sphinx." The Greeks having their legend of a winged woman with the body of a monster found a fanciful resemblance to her in this piece of ancient sculpture and called it the Sphinx.

The Reservoir of 1001 Columns. — This reservoir has not a drop of water in it, and is little more than a musty cellar with a few pillars dotted here and there. It was built by Constantine about the year 330, and had only 212 columns. The Orientals are fond of special numbers standing for an indefinite one. "Forty" and "1001" are good examples, as in the story of Ali Baba in the "Thousand Nights and One Night."

Kensington. — Kensington Palace is not in Kensington at all, but in the Westminster parish of St. Margaret. Westminster vestry draws £220 a year in rates from the Palace. Almost the whole of Kensington Gardens is in Westminster, and what does not belong to Westminster is within the parochial area of Paddington.

Palaces that are not Palaces. — Often the

name "palace," though sanctioned by the usage of the present century, is historically an error. Not every house occupied by a bishop becomes, *ipso facto*, a palace. " The term palace is, . strictly speaking, applicable only to the residence of a bishop in his cathedral city. We may properly speak of the palace at Wells, Chichester, Hereford, Lincoln, and the other places where the bishop lives under the shadow of his cathedral, but the name is misapplied to bishops' houses such as Fulham and Lambeth. They were manor houses and nothing more, and the prelates occupying them dated their letters 'from my manor house at Lambeth or Fulham,' etc., as the case might be."

Lambeth Palace, though occupied by the Archbishop of Canterbury, is not in its own diocese, but is in the diocese of Westminster. For more than a hundred and sixty years it was officially styled " Lambeth House." Previously Archbishop Laud, when he resided there, bestowed on it the title of Lambeth Manor. The residence of the Archbishop of York is sometimes called "the palace," but it was, and is, simply a manor house.

Westminster Abbey. — That venerable cornerstone of English history, " Westminster Abbey," has never been an abbey. It is the " church " of the Abbey of Westminster. The " Abbey," that is, the monastery, disappeared in the reign of Henry VIII. The legal title, since 1560, when Queen

Elizabeth replaced the Abbot by a Dean, is the " Collegiate Church of St. Peter,[1] in Westminster."

The " White " Tower. — From a Latin document of the year 1241 it appears that the great Norman keep, originally called Cæsar's Tower, the centre of the Tower of London, was called the " White " Tower from the coat of whitewash with which it was covered. Frowning, formidable, this " White " Tower rises with its four pinnacles above all the other sombre battlements of London's ancient citadel. Its walls are dark and gloomy, and behind them some of the blackest deeds in England's history have been done. And yet it is called " White."

Jack Straw's Castle. — On Hampstead Heath once existed a fortress known as Jack Straw's Castle. It was not a castle. It was a *hole* formed in the hillside on the site of the inn of the same name. Jack, who was one of the leaders in the Wat Tyler Insurrection, is said to have lived in it.

The " Apostles' Creed." — The " Apostles' Creed " is not of apostolic origin. " The tradition which [that] ascribes it to the Apostles themselves," says the Encyclopædia Britannica, " has no authority, and does not reach beyond the fifth century, if it can be carried so far. The definite source of the legend is supposed to be two sermons spuriously attributed to St. Augustine, and found in the appendix to his works." It is found

---

[1] Edward the Confessor's Church.

in the works of Ambrose, Bishop of Milan (374–397), but is supposed to have been included since his death.

"Nihilists" are Really "Radicals." — The term "Nihilist" was first used in Turgénief's "Fathers and Sons," where young Bazárof, asked what his creed was, replied: "I am a Nihilist— I believe in nothing." It was afterwards applied to those who advocated the abolition of all forms of government and the violent removal of rulers. Of course there are some even now to whom this signification would be appropriate, but they do not constitute the ruling majority of the Russian revolutionary party. The program given by Stepniak is thus set forth: Liberty in religious belief, freedom of the press and in public meeting, and government on the representative system. Surely this is not *nihil*. The program is not even republican in character. Stepniak says: "We all understand quite well that in contemporary Russia political liberty can be obtained only in the form of constitutional monarchy."

Workingmen are not "Proletarians." — According to the historical tradition, the sixth Roman king, Servius Tullius, divided the whole people into five *classes*, by means of a *census* or register of the inhabitants and their property, thus determining the tax (*tribulum*) which each citizen was to pay, the kind of military service he was to perform, and the position he would hold in the popular assembly. Each *classis* or army was divided into centuries. Those persons whose property did not amount to the minimum held by the members of the fifth *classis* (at least 10,000 copper *asses*, or about $150) formed a separate century consisting of three subdivisions, in the second of which were the *proletarii* or " begetters of children," their sole value consisting in the possibility of their furnishing offspring for the State. These had not less than 375 *asses*, they paid no taxes, and in time of danger might be armed at public expense. The word soon became a term of contempt, as of one supported at the cost of the community, hence a pauper. The word " proletarian " or " prolétaire " has of late years been unfortunately applied in the writings of Henry George and others to designate certain members of the working classes, wage earners, or day laborers. But it is absurd to call workingmen by such a title.

Don't call an Australian Black a " Native." — The descendants of the earlier settlers of Australia object to any one calling the black inhabitants " natives." The title in their opinion belongs only to them, and when applied to the " blacks " implies an insult. They claim that only the terms " aborigines " or " bushmen " should be used to signify the original inhabitants.

Lucifer is not Satan. — Lucifer as a popular name for Satan undoubtedly derives from Isaiah XIV., 12, which in the King James version reads:

"*How art thou fallen from heaven, O Lucifer, son of the morning!*" In the revised version the word Lucifer, which literally means " light-bringer," is rendered " day star." It is applied by Isaiah figuratively to a king of Babylon, but from this passage, and its resemblance to the account of the fallen archangel in the Talmud and in Milton's " Paradise Lost," the name was by the early church fathers also given to Satan. Milton nowhere calls Satan Lucifer, and the name in early times was borne by one of the popes, and also by a bishop of Cagliari in Sardinia, a separatist defender of the Nicene creed — the founder of the sect of Luciferians.

Why " Cabby " is a " Jehu." — The popular name for a London cabby is a " Jehu;" but as the original Jehu was a king of Israel, noted for his furious driving, this is a sarcastic appellation, what the rhetoricians call a *lucus a non lucendo*.

" Lord " Bacon a Misnomer. — Francis Bacon became Baron Verulam in 1618, and Viscount St. Albans in 1621, but the popular designation of him as " Lord " Bacon is incorrect.

" Bones " of Contention. — Many ignorant families, especially of foreign extraction, miscall their own names. Thus at one time the Des Isles pronounced their name " Desizzle." The L'Hommedieu family was called " the Lummydoos." The celebrated preacher and leather seller for whom the Parliament (of 1653) was deservedly named —

" Praise-God Barebones "—always subscribed himself Prayse Barbon.

Sunstroke not Chargeable to the Sun.—The common term " sunstroke," the effect of great heat, is a misnomer. " Heat apoplexy " would be more accurate, but not so convenient. Many persons suppose that it is caused only by direct exposure to the sun's rays. This is not so, for patients are frequently found in houses and barracks and tents, and at night as well as by day; and, whether in sun or shade, are generally those whose health is debilitated by dissipation, disease, and over-fatigue. Exposure to intense sun-rays is to be less feared in dry climates than in countries where the temperature is much lower, but the atmosphere is moist and perspiration is consequently retarded. People suffer more from a temperature of 87° Fahr. at Brussels, where the air is laden with moisture, than of 122° Fahr. at Cairo, where the air is extremely dry. General Greely says: " The inhabitants of the eastern coast of the United States hear with amazement of temperatures from 118° to 128° Fahr. being tolerated without harm in the dry region of Arizona and South Colorado, and that the ordinary avocations [*sic*] of farm and factory are pursued without inconvenience." This is due to the cooling effect of rapid evaporation from the surface of the body, and hence the sun's malignancy is unknown.

Stars do not " Fall " or " Shoot." — " Falling

stars " or " shooting stars " are not stars at all, but
meteors.   Stars are immense bodies, in many
cases larger than our sun, and revolving at such
enormous distances from us that their positions
remain relatively fixed.   Meteors are small bodies
— the vast majority weighing less than a pound each
— which in passing through our protecting atmosphere are subjected to such intense friction that
they are reduced to dust.   Only in rare cases do
they reach the earth.

**Gothic Architecture not invented by the
Goths.** — Gothic architecture, that is to say the
ecclesiastical architecture characterized by pointed
arches, is not in any way associated with the Goths.
The Italian renaissance writers applied the term
Goth or Gothic in contempt to that mediæval style
of building prevalent in certain parts of Europe,
just as they applied it to anything else that they
considered ugly or in bad taste.   In the literature
of a hundred years ago articles of native manufacture brought to England from New Zealand and
elsewhere were frequently called Gothic.

Venetian Glass. — Much of so-called Venetian
glass is not made in Venice, but in Murano.   The
word "Venetian" may perhaps be considered as
derived from the province of Veneto, of which
Venice is the capital, but of which Murano was
the ancient seat.

Dresden China in Dresden. — The Royal Dresden china is not made at Dresden, but at a gov-

ernment factory at Meissen thirteen miles farther down the Elbe; but by a fair exchange Meissen ware is manufactured at Dresden.

Dutch Clocks. — Dutch clocks are all "made in Germany," chiefly at Freyburg, in the Black Forest. Dutch is only our way of mispronouncing *Deutsch*, by which the Germans call their own language.

"Chamois" Leather a Sham. — Our German silver (which, by the way, is not of German origin, but has been known in China for centuries) we clean with leather which is called chamois or "chammy skin." This leather is not derived from the chamois, — which, if we may believe the redoubtable Tartarin of Tarascon, is an all but extinct quadruped, — but is the flesh side of sheepskin, reduced to an even thickness with pumice stone, and soaked in lime water and a solution of sulphuric acid. After being fulled with wooden hammers, fish oil is poured over it. This process is several times repeated, and after careful washing in a solution of potash, it is wrung, dried, made supple by stretching, and finally polished by rolling. The word itself may be derived from the Swedish *samsk* or the Romany *chamische*, meaning leather. Others derive it from the Dutch *sam*, soft.

Camel's-hair, Moleskin, and Catgut. — Camelhair paint-brushes are all made from the hair of the squirrel, and mole-skin is a strong cotton fabric of fustian, having a soft, smooth surface.

The little strip that fastens the fish-hook to a line
is really silk. The manufacture is carried on in
Spain. When the silkworms are about to spin,
they are thrown into tubs of vinegar and left there
some time. When sufficiently pickled they are
carefully opened by women and children, who take
out the glutinous unspun silk and draw it into
strands about two feet long. These are left to dry,
and the particles of the worm are rubbed off. After
the wrinkled ends — about half of the strand — are
cut off, they are tied up into bunches with colored
wool and sent to all parts of the world. We call it
catgut. The "catgut" used for stringed instruments is made from the intestines of sheep.

Frauds in the Larder. — So-called "soluble"
cocoas are really only miscible; orange "marmalade," according to the purists, has nothing of the
nature of real marmalade about it except its
color, and should simply be called orange jam, for
they say real marmalade is made from the quince,
called by the Portuguese *marmelo*, and when made
into jam, *marmelada;* the word is derived from the
Greek *mĕli*, honey, and *melon*, an apple.

Cream of tartar has no cream in it; black lead is
not lead at all, but is a compound of carbon and iron,
another form of soot, or charcoal, or diamond,
whichever is preferred; for these, including black
lead, are all chemically the same substance, though
in different forms. The ordinary "quart" bottle
will only hold one pint and a third instead of two

pints.   The sealing " wax" with which it is sealed does not contain a particle of wax, but is compounded from shellac and Venice turpentine.

Country Dances. — This dance denotes no reference to the country.   It is properly a " contra" dance, from the French *contredanse*.   De Quincey argues in favor of retaining the corruption, since it has taken root in the language.

Cork Legs. — There is no trace of cork about a cork leg, apart from the name.   The name arises from the fact that nearly all the great manufacturers of such articles were established in Cork street, Piccadilly.   Nevertheless the latest dictionaries declare that cork is frequently used in the manufacture of artificial limbs.   Papier maché is the substance now chiefly used, at least in America, for that purpose.

CHAPTER II.

MISTAKES WE MAKE ABOUT PLACES.

Ice in Iceland. — One would conclude, from the name only, that Iceland is a land of ice. It is no more so than Greenland is a land of verdure. On the contrary, it is a land of abundant meadows, sustaining great flocks of horned sheep and herds of cattle and ponies, and producing potatoes, cabbages, and turnips. Extremes of temperature are unknown in Iceland. There are glaciers, but they form no icebergs, and the sea around the island is never frozen. Owing to the Gulf stream the climate is mild in winter and balmy in summer, yet is just insufficiently favorable for the maturing of corn and fruit.

Cold Winters. — Yakutsk is not the coldest town on earth; this distinction belongs to Vercho-yansk in the same locality, which, according to the report of the Geological Society of St. Petersburg, holds the record of minus 67° centigrade. The reading of the thermometer gives a very exaggerated impression of the severity of low temperatures. The author of "Twenty Years on the Saskatchewan," writing from Edmonton (Alberta in Canada), says: "I have known the temperature so mild that the birds have been singing most of the time, and very little extra clothes have been worn; and again for weeks together the glass has been between 36° and 50° below zero. Yet our cold winters have been the healthiest and the succeeding summers generally the most fruitful."

The Roof of the World. — The name *Pamir* is Russian and means " On [top of] the world." But the highest land is now believed to be the Chang plateau, lying north of and running nearly parallel to the head-waters of the Western Brahmapootra, or Sango. This might well be called " The Roof of the World."

Fuji-yama. — The beautiful snow-capped peak of Central Japan, Fuji, so often pictured in Kakemonos and prints, is frequently seen under the form Fuji-yama or Fuji-san. Either affix means *mountain*. It is therefore tautological to say " the remarkable mountain of Fuji-yama." There are many " yamas " in Japan, there is only one Fuji in the world; and that name is also given out of compliment to Japan's famous warship.

Mistakes about other Mountains. — It is a common impression that Mount Blanc is in Switzerland. It is wholly within the French frontier province of Haute Savoie. Mount St. Elias is not the highest mountain in North America; there are two if not three peaks in the Mt. St. Elias region of Alaska known to be higher than St. Elias. The highest is about 19,500 feet. A peak about 1,500 feet higher is named after Sir William " Logan," founder of the Canadian Geological Survey. Both of these mountains are in British territory, as has been confirmed since 1887 by the Canada-Alaska Boundary Survey. The usual statement that Mount Ararat was the place on which Noah's ark rested has no foundation in the Hebrew text, which reads: " On the mountains of Ararat." Ararat was the ancient name of a *district* in Eastern Armenia, and has been used for all Armenia.

In this connection it may be interesting to give the greatest altitudes in each State in the Union.

GREATEST ALTITUDES IN EACH STATE.

FROM THE RECORDS OF THE UNITED STATES GEOLOGICAL SURVEY.

STATE OR TERRITORY.	Name of Place.	Height.
Alabama	Cheauha Mt. (Talladega Co.)..	2,407
Alaska	(Not named)	19,500
Arizona	San Francisco Mt.............	12,794
Arkansas	Magazine Mt.................	2,800
California	Mt. Whitney	14,898
Colorado......	Blanca Peak	14,464
Connecticut...	Bear Mt.....................	2,355
Delaware.....	Dupont	282
D. of Columbia	Tenley	400
Florida........	Highland	210
Georgia	Enota Mt....................	4,798
Idaho	Mead Peak [1]	10,541

[1] Salmon River mountains, known to be much higher, but the elevation is not definitely known.

STATE OR TERRITORY.	Name of Place.	Height.
Illinois	Warren...................	1,009
Indian Territ'y.	Wichita Mts...............	2,500
Indiana........	Haley...................	1,140
Iowa	Ocheyedan...............	1,554
Kansas	Kanarado...............	3,906
Kentucky.....	Big Black Mt. (Harlan Co.)...	4,100
Louisiana	Mansfield	321
Maine	Katahdin Mt. (Kataadn).......	5,200
Maryland.....	Great Backbone Mt...........	3,400
Massachusetts.	Mt. Greylock	5,535
Michigan	Porcupine Mt.................	2,023
Minnesota	Woodstock................	1,826
Mississippi....	Pontotic Ridge	566
Missouri......	Cedar Gap	1,675
Montana	Mt. Douglas................	11,300
Nebraska.....	White River Summit..........	4,876
Nevada.......	Wheeler Peak..............	13,036
N. Hampshire.	Mount Washington	6,286
New Jersey ...	Kittatinny Mountain	1,630
New Mexico ..	Cerro Blanco..............	14,269
New York	Mt. Marcy (Adirondack)......	5,379
North Carolina.	Mt. Mitchell................	6,703
North Dakota.	Sentinel Butte...............	2,707
Ohio	Ontario	1,376
Oklahoma.....	Goodwin	2,536
Oregon	Mt. Hood................	11,225
Pennsylvania .	Negro Mt..................	2,826
Rhode Island .	Durfee Hill	805
South Carolina.	Rocky Mt. (Pickens Co.)......	3,600
South Dakota.	Harney Peak................	7,368
Tennessee	Mt. Leconte................	6,612
Texas	North Franklin Mt...........	7,069
Utah	Mt. Emmons...............	13,694
Vermont	Mt. Mansfield	4,430
Virginia	Mt. Rogers (Grayson Co.)	5,719

State or Territory.	Name of Place.	Height.
Washington...	Mt. Rainier	14,444
West Virginia.	Spruce Mt. (Pendleton Co.)....	4,860
Wisconsin	Summit Lake	1,732
Wyoming.....	Fremont Peak.................	13,790

Unter den Linden. — An 1897 geography describes the most famous thoroughfare in Berlin, Unter den Linden (under the lime-trees), as "a wide, open drive, with six parallel rows of shady lime-trees running along." The truth is, the lime-trees are so few, and so insignificant, that the name now signifies nothing.

Scottish "Shires" are Misnomers. — In most newspapers that portion of Scotland properly called Sutherland is misnamed Sutherlandshire. One may as well write Northumberlandshire or Cornwallshire. *Shire* is essentially Anglo-Saxon, and ought to distinguish exclusively a Saxon occupation of certain parts of England, not of Scotland, where the Saxons never went. To this loose way of using *shire* the allotropic condition of "Argyleshire" is due. The first part of the word, meaning "the land of the Gael," shows it to be a memorial of Irish colonizations, but the affix makes it the land of the Saxon.

Such names as Devonshire and Merionethshire are not entitled to the retention of *shire*, for the

Saxons never occupied any considerable portion of the first, or penetrated the second.

Jutland. — Many take it for granted, because of the suggestive spelling, that this Danish peninsula is so named on account of its *jutting* out into the sea. There is no connection between these words, not properly even in the sound, for the signification is that this land formerly belonged to the Jutes, and the correct pronunciation is *Yoot*-land.

Holland. — More than one school geography states that the word Holland means "hollow land." Skeat's etymological dictionary gives the same derivation, adding that it means "low-lying." Littré derives it from *hohl* and *land*, with the same signification. The same authority mentions the theory that it comes from *holt*, meaning *wood;* thence an island on which Dortrecht is situated, and by extension the whole land; again, it may come from Helium or Helle, the ancient name of one of the mouths of the Meuse, Holland for Hel-land.

Oxford and the Bosporos. — This word is compounded from *bous*, a bullock, cow, or ox, and *poros*, a passage. This suggests the fallacious etymological derivation of the English Oxford — the ford of the oxen, which is from the Keltic *nisga*, water, and *ford*. The Greek myth that Io, changed into a white cow by Zeus, was chased over the world by a gad-fly sent by the jealous Here caused several straits to be named Bosporos. The best known are the Thracian, the Kimmerian, and the Indian.

Morea. — The name given in modern geography to the ancient Peloponnesus (Southern Greece) is derived from the Slavonic *more*, the "sea," and not from a word which indicates its fancied resemblance to a mulberry leaf, as taught in hundreds of schools every day. The Morea is more deeply indented by the sea than any other European country. The same root is found in the word Pomerania, which means "on the sea."

Gaul. — This word did not in ancient times designate merely the country now called France; historical class-books lead one to suppose that it did. As, at the present time, Britain includes Scotland and Wales as well as England, so Gaul in Roman times included Belgium and Switzerland as well as France. "All Gaul is divided into three parts," says Cæsar in the first sentence of his "Commentaries."

Babylon and Babel. — Popular etymology deduces the meaning of these names from the Hebrew "confusion," after the explanation of Gen. XI., 9. Webster's Dictionary says Babel is "for *balbel*, from *balal*, to mix, confound;" but it adds that "it is more probably a contraction from *beth* and *bel*, the house of Belus, equivalent to Baal," but the word in the cuneiform inscriptions is Ca-dimirra, the Semitic translation of which is *bab-ili* or *bab-El*, "Gate of God."

Calvary.—The Gospels do not confirm the assertion that the place of our Lord's crucifixion bore the specific name of Mount Calvary. The word "Calvary" in Luke XXIII., 33, is from the Latin word *calvarium*, which means a skull, and is the same in significance as the Hebrew *gugo leth*; possibly, therefore, a bald hill (Latin *calvus*, bald).

Baffin Bay is not a Bay.—Of names "writ in water" none could be more inappropriate than Baffin Bay, which not even in shape is a bay, but is an immense inland sea, much larger than the Mediterranean Sea, and having nearly six times the area of the Black Sea.

Hudson Bay.—Hudson "Bay," which is scarcely smaller than Baffin "Bay," should also be called a sea. "Hudson's Bay" is the way it is spelt in literature, yet on any map the spelling is always Hudson Bay.

Nelson River.—The great Nelson River is not named after the naval hero, but after another British sailor of the same name, the master of one of Sir T. Button's ships, who died and was buried there in 1612.

Bering Strait.—The strait generally called Behring should be Bering Strait. The South Kensington Natural History Museum specimens from this region are all labelled "Bering," after the Danish navigator, Bering, who proved that Asia and America are separated. He died on Bering

Island, in the Bering Sea. It is thus officially recognized by the United States Government.

There were Thirty-nine Cinque Ports. — Cinque is French for " five," and originally there were only five ports forming a confederacy that maintained a royal navy on outpost duty. But shortly after the Conquest two others were added in Kent and Sussex. From time to time thirty-two other ports joined the association, making in all thirty-nine, but the name " Cinque " was still retained.

Korea. — Corea is more accurately spelt with a " K "—Korea. Such is the official spelling originally promulgated by the Royal Geographical Society. The kingdom was originally called in Chinese " Korai," which is an abbreviation of Ko-Korai, its founder, who obtained the mastery about the sixth century. But for hundreds of years, ever since the complete overthrow of this kingdom by the founders of the present one, that name has been discarded. It would be far better to have adopted the native name Cho-sen, not, however, with any implication that they are the chosen people.

The Blarney Stone. — It is said that in 1825 Sir Walter Scott, while on a tour through the South of Ireland, kissed the Blarney Stone, as thousands of tourists imagine they do every year.

The wonder-working stone — a block bearing the name of the founder of Blarney Castle, and the date of 1446 — is built into the south angle of

the keep, twenty feet below the top, and outside.
Since access to it is well-nigh impossible, a substitute *within* the battlements is imposed on the credu-
lous. But for visitors who insist on leaning over
the edge, supported by the heels, there is yet
another *real* stone, dated 1703.

A Desert that is Fertile. — The Kalahari
" desert" is not the waste of sand and stone that
a typical desert should be. According to Mr. J. T.
Bent, author of " The Ruined Cities of Mashonaland," it is " a vast undulating expanse of country
covered with timber — the mimosa or camel-thorn,
the mapani-bush, and others which reach the water
with their roots, though there are no ostensible
water sources above the ground. Wild animals
rapidly becoming extinct elsewhere abound there-
in." We read further on that the wild tribes
exhibit great skill in finding the water when the
season is dry, " by suction through a reed inserted
in the ground, the results being spat into a gourd
and handed to the thirsty traveller to drink."
Many other so-called deserts abound in wild shrubs
or grass, and require only systematic irrigation to
become veritable gardens.

Sodom and Gomorrah. — Scientific researches
tell us that the traditionary sites of the cities of
Sodom and Gomorrah, covered by the Dead Sea,
are geologically impossible.

Arabia Felix. — That part of Arabia called
Felix, or the Happy, was called by the Arabs

Yemen, meaning the land to the right of Mecca. The Latin writers took it in the sense of *dexter*, fortunate; hence Felix, happy.

Antwerp. — The heraldic cognizance of Antwerp is said to be two hands referring to the popular derivation of the city's name: from *handt werpen*, hand throwing, referring to the manufactured legend that a giant named Antigonus cut off the right hands of travellers that could not pay toll, and threw them into the river Skeld. The name comes really from *aan* and *werf:* " at the wharf."

Belgrade. — The name of this town is not French as some have supposed, but is Slavonic, from *bieli*, white, and *gorod* or *grad*, town. It therefore means the white town. But the name white as applied to the Tsar of Russia is a literal translation of the Mongol town Tchagan Khan, which in turn is from the Chinese character Hwang, which means self-ruler, autocrat; but by a slight mistake in making the character, the symbol for *self* became the symbol for *white*.

Cambridge not the Bridge on the Cam. — It is generally supposed that the name Cambridge is the bridge on the Cam. It is really a contraction of Cambo-rit-um, its ancient name, which means " the ford of the *Cam rhyd* or crooked river.

Red Sea. — The Hebrew for this inland sea is Yam Sùph, sea of bulrushes. The name Red may refer to the color of the neighboring inhabitants.

Gates Misunderstood. — The English name Aldgate should properly be Algate, meaning free to all. Cripplegate also is wrongly understood as referring to a gate frequented by beggars. It was a covered way leading to the barbican. It is odd that Billingsgate, which commemorates the Anglo-Saxon term " family of the Gods," should come to mean the rough language of the slums. Grubstreet is not named because of its eating-houses, but perhaps because a *grube*, or ditch, may have once been there.

Marylebone. — This familiar church is not so called from Marie la Bonne as some have supposed, but from Mary le Bourne, meaning the chapel of St. Mary on the bourne or brook. It was the same brook that is perpetuated in Tyburn.

Mt. Pilatus not Named after Pilate. — The beautiful mountain near Lucerne did not derive its name from Pontius Pilate having drowned himself in the lake near its top. Pilatus should be Pileatus, the cloud-*capped*. In the same way Chapeau Dieu near the Bay of Fundy became Shepody Mountain. Neither does Monte Rosa, as Wordsworth says, take its name " from roseate hues far kenned at morn and even." It comes from the Keltic *ros*, a peak.

Gramercy Park. — The name of this quiet oasis in New York is not French as some suppose, but is derived from the Dutch De Kromme Zee, " the crooked pond," which once occupied its site.

What a City really Is. — The term city in the

United Kingdom is generally applied to a town which is incorporated, and which is, or was, the seat of a bishop or the capital of his See; yet it does not necessarily follow that it must contain a cathedral.

St. Peter's at Rome. — St. Peter's at Rome is generally supposed to be the chief church of that city, but St. John Lateran is the cathedral of Rome, the Metropolitan Church of its bishops, and, as the inscription on its statue-laden façade asserts, "Mother and head of all churches in the city and the world."

CHAPTER III.

MISTAKES WE MAKE ABOUT PLANTS.

Botanical Misnomers. — The "African" marigold is a native of Mexico; the tuberose has nothing of the rose about it, being simply a tuberous plant, and the name is a corruption of the Latin *tuberosa*, knobby; "French" beans originally came from India; toadstools have nothing whatever to do with toads, the name being either a mistaken application or humorous perversion of the German *tod* and *stuhl*, meaning death-stool, in reference to the poisonous nature of these fungi; and the "Jerusalem" artichoke (*Helianthus tuberosus*) is a native of Peru. Introduced by the Italians, it was at first called *girasole articiocco*, which Englishmen quickly pronounced in the usual way. A *girasole* is a sunflower, which the artichoke closely resembles. The word artichoke comes from the Arabic *alkharshúf*.

Coffee "Berry." — The coffee "berry" is not a berry, but a seed. The fruit of the coffee tree is a berry which has the shape and color of a ripe cherry, and it would puzzle most persons to distinguish a heap of real coffee berries from the edible fruit. Each berry contains two seeds, lying with the flat sides together, and these, after having been removed from the double husk, are prepared for market.

Briar Pipes. — Briar pipes are not made from the wood of the briar, but from the *bruyère*, or white Mediterranean heather root.

Rice Paper. — The rice plant contributes nothing but the name to the manufacture of " rice " cigarette-papers. " Rice " paper is made only from perfectly new trimmings of linen, and comes mostly from English and French mills in Constantinople, Fumen (in Austria), and France. Chinese rice paper is made from thin slices of the pith of a tree cane that grows about five feet high. A sharp knife pares the pith into cylinders of uniform thickness, which are then unrolled and pressed out into so-called " rice " paper.

Egyptian Cigarettes and Tobacco. — Since 1890 the cultivation of the tobacco plant in Egypt has been prohibited. The Cairenes are justly celebrated for workmanship and the curing of the leaf, but the tobacco they import comes entirely from Turkey.

Deer Forests are without Trees. — A deer " forest" may be without a tree or even a shrub. The origin of the word can be traced through the Italian *foresta* or old French *forest* to the Low Latin *forestum*, and it is connected with the classical Latin *foras* (out doors), from *foris* a door, from which we get our word " foreign," meaning " external." A forest is, in fact, a piece of land placed out of cultivation; to afforest a tract is to place it so, and to disafforest is to declare that it may again be cultivated. It was for hunting deer that the tracts of land were so placed; and because these frequently contained a large number of trees, a mistaken notion grew up that the words "forest" and "woods" were synonymous.

Why Trees Split. — The splitting of forest trees by frost is ascribed to the same cause as the bursting of water-pipes; namely, the expansion of the sap turning into ice. This is not the case. The splitting is due to the contraction of the wood by frost, similar, but in a less degree, to what happens when the wood is dried. When the thaw comes the trees expand to their original dimensions. "After a number of years' measurements," according to the London "Chronicle," "Mr. Clayton, of Bradford, finds that the difference between the girths in October, just before the frost, and February, when the thermometer was below freezing, ranges for different trees from two-sixteenths to six-sixteenths of an inch."

The Movement of Sap. — There is no truth in the belief that "sap goes down in the winter and up in the spring." As a matter of fact, the water in trees increases from the time the leaves wither, and all through the winter until early spring. The branches in winter are almost saturated with water. The sap does not "go up" until the warm weather evaporates the stored-up moisture through the already expanded foliage.

The Banyan. — A remarkably persistent error is that banyan branches spread

> " so broad and long that in the ground
> The bended twigs take root, and daughters grow
> About the mother tree."

When Milton wrote these words about this wonderful fig-tree he had, of course, read Pliny's account, and then copied his error about the bended twigs taking root. Tales to the same effect were plentifully supplied in London before Milton's time, by servants of the Honorable East Indian Company returning to tell of the strange things they had seen. The facts are these: as the *Ficus bengalensis* . spreads over such a great area and is in leaf during the hottest season, the consequent evaporation would soon exhaust it unless it were replenished by other means than the main column; the roots sent down for this purpose do not defeat their own aim, as is so commonly taught, and become parent trees, but are supports for the tree's enormously long branches, and crutches to itself in its old age.

Rosewood Trees. — There is a mistaken impression that rosewood takes its name from its color. Rosewood is not red or yellow, but almost black. Its name comes from the fact that when first cut it exhales a perfume similar to that of the rose; and although the dried rosewood of com-

merce retains no trace of this early perfume, the
name lingers.

Mummy Wheat. — There is no foundation for
the belief that wheat 2,000 years old will come to
life. The stories of wheat found inside sarcophagi
and mummy cases germinating after thousands of
years have been proved unauthentic times out of
number by Hooker, Carruthers, Flinders-Petrie,
Newberry, and every other botanist and antiquary
of any eminence, and likewise by committees of
the British Association and the United States Department of Agriculture. Wheat seldom preserves
its vitality beyond the eighth or ninth year. In
the "Standard" lately appeared a letter from Mr.
Newberry, who says that out of the seeds of thirty
species of plants found by him in similar situations
not one sprouted. His latest failure was with
three peach-stones — probably of Roman date —
disinterred from a tomb at Beni Hasan, in Upper
Egypt. The fact is the seeds, like the mummies,
have been oxidized to the centre. At the South
Kensington Health Exhibition there was shown a
model of the Roman baths uncovered at Bath, and
in the centre stood a large seed-pan filled with
ferns, with a label attached stating that they were
grown from seeds (spores) obtained from fern
leaves during the excavations, and found so many
feet under the Roman ruins, where they had lain
so many hundreds of years — and the public believed it!

Primroses and other Flowers. — Primroses when planted upside down sometimes come up and display a different color. This is not the effect of eccentric planting, for flowers of a different color often appear on the wayside primrose when it is transferred to a garden in the ordinary way. The same change may be observed in the color of other flowers, and depends on several causes; the nature of the soil is one. A well-known instance is that of the hydrangea, the color of whose flower is changed from pink to blue by a specially prepared soil, or in some districts by the natural soil of the garden. One carnation plant will produce blooms of several different colors.

The Aloe. — A gardeners' fable makes the aloe live a century before it flowers. In the Scilly Islands aloes that arrive at maturity and die before a fifth of this time may be seen any day. Indeed, in some places they flower and then die even in the tenth year.

The Lotus. — The lotus, the sacred plant of the Egyptians, symbolizing the northern part of their country as the papyrus did the southern, did not grow in the Nile. It was cultivated in ponds and tanks, and in the sacred lakes attached to the temples. The only places where it is still found are some pools, principally in the Delta. The annual rise and fall of the water render its existence in the stream itself all but impossible.

Gutta-percha. — The gum called gutta-percha

is not from the Latin *gutta*, a drop, but is a bastard spelling of the Malayan name *gotah pertcha*; that is, " gum of Sumatra," whence it was originally obtained.

Hawthorn. — Hawthorn is not a thorn that bears haws, but one that grows in the haw or hedge.

Hollyhocks a Sort of Hoax. — The hollyhock has nothing to do etymologically with either the holly or the oak. Hock is old English for mallow, and when the flower was introduced from the Holy Land it was given its name, the Holi-hoc; it is sometimes called rose-mallow, or the outre-mer rose. It is a native of China.

Wormwood not a Wood for Worms. — Professor Skeat shows that wormwood is not, as was formerly supposed, compounded of two Anglo-Saxon words meaning to keep off maggots, but is wermod, meaning mind-preserver.

Gooseberries not for Geese. — The delicious fruit, so prized in Scotland, but elsewhere somewhat despised on account of its name, has no association with the goose! Its name may be from the *goss* or *gorse*, a prickly plant; but more likely from gooseberry, *groiseberry*, allied with the middle high German *grus*, curling, crisped.

CHAPTER IV.

MISTAKES WE MAKE ABOUT ANIMALS.

"Mad Dog!" — A rabid dog never foams at the mouth. A fit, usually brought on by over-exertion in running, will sometimes produce this effect; the remedy should be cold water to the animal's head. The name " hydrophobia " means the fear of water, and the belief that mad dogs dread water having become general, the sight of a dog eagerly lapping water and even plunging into it leads people to exclaim, " He drinks! There is no danger." Yet burning thirst is one of the characteristics of rabies in its early stages.

Dog-days and Rabies. — "Dog-days" have no more to do with rabies than the moon has to do with lunacy. Dogs are liable to attacks in every month of the year, but the fewest cases occur in July and August. The records of the veterinary schools of Alfort, Toulouse, Paris, London, and Lyons show that a majority of cases occur in the wettest months. In April, November, and December the recorded cases are double and triple those in June, July, and August. In hot countries the disease is rare, and in some even unknown.

The Bloodhound. — The bloodhound is not nat-

turally cruel. He is trained to scent blood. His
mission is to track, not to injure. Fugitives are
rarely, if ever, torn or injured by him when he
brings them to bay.

The Bull-dog not so Ugly as he is Ugly. — The
bull-dog is a living contradiction to the assertion
that character can be told by the face. He is not
savage, stupid, or treacherous. There is no authen-
tic instance of one attacking a man unprovoked.
His ugliness lies in his phiz *and not* in his temper,
and it arises from the fact that the lower canine
teeth are in front of the upper canine teeth.

Cat's Eyes are not Phosphorescent. — A cat's
eyes do not shine in the dark; that is to say, in the
total absence of light. A body must be luminous
to shine in darkness, and no creature possesses
light-giving eyes. Pussy's eyes appear to be bright
in the dark because the widely distended pupil
catches what light there is, thus collecting rays which
are invisible to us; so her eyes seem to shine with
a light of their own.

The King of Beasts a Coward. — The lion has
been accredited with immense strength, courage,
and almost nobility of character. African travellers, such as Livingstone, Baker, and Selous, show
that these attributes are fictitious. The so-called
king of beasts is a cowardly, skulking brute, which
would much rather run away than fight, unless it
can take its enemy unaware, or is rendered desperate by hunger. Its nature is to be sleepy all day,

and to dislike exertion in broad daylight, especially after a night's gorging on an antelope.

The lion has also a worldwide fame for the possession of a cavernous mouth.

> " Van Amburgh is the man
>   Who goes to all the shows;
>   He puts his head in the lion's mouth
>   And tells you what he knows."

Thus runs the poem, but no lion or tiger ever had a mouth big enough to admit the human head.

In strength it is inferior to other members of its family. Its forepaws have only sixty-nine per cent. and its hind legs only sixty-five per cent. respectively of the muscular power possessed by those of the tiger.

Bison. — " Buffalo Bill " and his companions are said to have killed 4,280 " buffaloes " in eighteen months, that the laborers on the Kansas Pacific Railway might be provided with meat. But from a naturalist's standpoint, they did nothing of the kind: all their " buffaloes " were bison. The true buffalo is found only in the Old World; it is domesticated generally in India and Southern Asia, whence it was introduced into Egypt and Southern Europe. In the wild state it inhabits the Indian jungles. The wild and fiercer Cape buffalo is an analogous species.

The name Aurochs (Latin *Urus*) is sometimes incorrectly applied to the bison. The Aurochs was

a gigantic prehistoric animal from which it is commonly believed that the wild Chillingham cattle,
though much inferior in size, are descended, probably after domestication and interbreeding. A few
specimens of the Aurochs are still preserved in
Lithuania and the Caucasus. A few specimens of
the American bison are also to be found in the
Yellowstone Park and in one or two private preserves.

How a Bull charges. — In almost every drawing in which a cow, bison, or buffalo is seen charg-
ing a man, the animal is represented with its horns
lowered, however far away it may be from the
intended victim. This horned animals never do
until they are at close quarters, for were they to do
so their sight would not aid them, and their enemy
would probably escape.

The Ship of the Desert. — The camel is usually
cited as the most notable example of ability to
endure thirst. Sir C. Rivers Wilson says that none
of the camels that had been without water from six
to seven days on the march to Abu Klea survived,
and that to keep them in good condition it is necessary to water them at least every second day.
There is no truth in the statement that the camel
carries a water reservoir in its stomach, or that the
Bedouins, if they are near death from thirst, kill
the camel and drink the water stored in the stomach. In the desert these fables are unknown.

Mice and Marmots. — If one wants a type of

abstinence from water the common mouse may be chosen. They have been known to live in a warm room for three and a half months without having any drink, and, while eating heartily of dry maize and grass seeds, to seem quite equal to prolonging their water-fast for a month or two more. The seals in Bering Sea go without food or water for three or four months, subsisting on their own fat; and bears, while hibernating, of course neither eat nor drink. It was at one time supposed that the prairie dog in the Western deserts went long without water, but it has been recently discovered that the intelligent little creatures dig wells so deep that they reach water level. The prairie dog, though it barks, is not a dog, but a rodent; belonging to the same family as the woodchuck.

It may be well here to add that the "shrew-mouse" is not a mouse or akin to a mouse. Its name comes from the Anglo-Saxon *scredwa* from the verb scearfa, to gnaw. Neither does it in biting cattle cause any peculiar malady. In the same iconoclastic spirit we may dispel any lingering notion that a guinea-pig is a pig, or that it comes from Guinea. It is a rodent, and its home is South America.

The Monkey and the Stick. — Why is the ourang-outang represented pictorially with a stick? What would he do with it in the thick undergrowth of his tropical home, and where would he put it while climbing the branches overhead? The ourang cannot stand upright or turn round without the free support of both arms, and he seldom descends to the ground, but passes from tree to tree, often at great altitudes, walking along the larger limb of one till he reaches the boughs of the next, from which he swings to another, and so proceeds, mile after mile, over a continuous interwoven highway.

Coneys are not Rabbits. — The coney of Scripture is not our "bunny." Preachers are sometimes guilty of confounding the two. The animal mentioned in Psalm CIV. is supposed to be the daman, the Syrian hyrax, a small-hoofed mammal with rhinoceros-like molars. Its cousins at the Cape are miscalled rock-badgers.

The Sloth not Slothful. — The "sloth" is an expert climber, full of life, and traverses the branches of forest trees at a speed which is anything but slothful. He does not descend to the ground, for his long limbs and curved claws are not adapted for standing. The sloth on the ground will not take more than thirty steps a day, and will not go a mile in a month. His native name is Aï. He used to be considered imperfect and deformed.

Names that are Fur-fetched. — Ermine is the symbol of justice, and its whiteness makes it a choice fur for maidens to wear; but the "ermine" is merely the reddish-brown stoat in its winter dress. Like so many animals which inhabit northern latitudes, the stoat changes in the winter to an almost complete white; the tail alone remains black.

The polar bear, we are continually told, "is

always white like the snow." But as he grows old he grows brown, and the whale fishers nickname him " Old Brownie."

Frauds in Fur. — Many furs bearing high-sounding names are really derived from humble creatures. Mink goes under the name of American sable. Skunk is " black martin " till it gets out; then its odor tells its origin. The muskrat or " musquash " masquerades as brook otter. The coney, subjected to an electric process to remove its long hairs, becomes a French seal; and so people deceive themselves.

The Beaver. — The beaver, it is asserted, always cuts the tree so that it may fall toward the water. Trees growing near the water lean toward a stream or pond, and the heaviest branches grow over where light and space are greatest; the larger number of those cut by the beavers would naturally fall in that direction; moreover the animals coming up out of the water would first gnaw on that side.

Beavers do not use their tails as a trowel, but only to propel them through the water and to slap down the mud and soft earth. The beaver selects the trees above his dam; and when the water is swift builds it diagonally. He carries his building materials between his forepaws and chin, arranges them with his forepaws, and slaps with his flat tail. They do not drive in piles.

Sealskin that is not Sealskin. — The commonly known " sealskin " is not furnished by the true seal,

whose skin is almost useless except when used as
an ornamental mat or stiff rug. It is the sea-lions
and bears, the eared seals, *Otaria*, whose skins are
so highly valued because so soft and warm. The
skins on the living animals have not, as is often supposed, the same downy appearance as they have
when they are ready for clothing, being covered
with long, coarse, deep-rooted hairs, which drop
out when dressed by the furrier, and leave the soft,
woolly hair uninjured.

Seals are not flayed Alive. — A diatribe headed
" Fashion and Sealskin " in an evening paper says :
" Surely fifty or a hundred guineas could not possibly be better spent than purchasing every now
and then a skin that has been *torn from the living
animal*; most suitable apparel for the 'gentle'
sex ! " Says another serious writer of fiction in one
of the weeklies : " The sealskin jacket represents
some half-dozen dams who have been skinned
alive, while their little ones have been left to starve
in all the slow agonies of starvation." The cruelty
exists in the writer's imagination. Mother seals,
technically called *cows*, are not slaughtered, but
only the " bachelors " which are about four years
old and have no little ones. What really takes place
happens hourly in every slaughter-house in the
world. After the skins of cattle are removed, the
flesh quivers for some time. The reports of the
United States Fish Commission describe the process : " At a given signal down comes the club,

and the seal is stunned and motionless; their skulls, being very thin, are easily fractured. This operation being over, the men seize the prostrate seals by the hind flippers, and range them in rows. Then each sealer takes his knife and drives it into the heart, and any slight movement of the animal soon ceases. Then follows the skinning.".

It would be a dangerous operation for one man, and much too expensive to employ several, to flay a live seal, often eight feet in length, and with teeth surpassing those of the largest dog.

Whales do not spout Water. — The whale is not a fish; it differs from its fishy neighbors in breathing, as man does, by lungs; in having warm blood and no scales; in having a four-chambered heart (fishes have two chambers); and particularly in the fact that its young are born alive and nourished with milk. Nor do they spout water as they are always represented doing in pictures, wherein the column always takes the form of a glorious fountain. They breathe out the heated air of the lungs, and as they begin to do so just before they approach the surface, the effort results in the water just above the nostrils on the top of the head being carried up into the air in the form of a jet; while the heated breath being condensed by sudden exposure to the outer cold appears in the form of fine spray or vapor. The whale's nostrils are guarded by valvular structures which close when under water, and prevent it from penetrating.

Flying-fish and Squirrels. — Flying-fish have no wings, but long extended fins, used simply to sustain them like a parachute. Some persons imagine that they flap these to lengthen their leaps through the air. This is wrong. Their fins are motionless from the time they leap from the sea till they drop into it again. The leaping of the flying-squirrel, which has the skin of the sides very much extended between the fore and hind legs, is analogous.

Small Fry. — The sardine, whitebait, and morris are not distinct species. The sardine develops into pilchard, the whitebait is the young of the herring and the sprat, and the mysterious morris only the conger in another stage of life.

Are Zebras Untamable? — The striped zebra, which makes such a picturesque part of a circus, is generally supposed to be untamable. But Baron Walter Rothschild, of London, after long experiments succeeded in getting together a team of four, which he drives without trouble.

CHAPTER V.

BIRDS AND INSECTS.

Birds with Wrong Names. — The plural of mouse is mice. Analogy misled our English ancestors to imagine that the singular of grice (the distinctively gray bird) must be grouse! Bryant thus speaks, in " The Old Man's Counsel," of the different names by which the grouse is known in this country :

> " I listened, and from midst the depth of woods
> Heard the love-signal of the grouse, that wears
> A sable ruff around his mottled neck ;
> Partridge they call him by our Northern streams,
> And pheasant by the Delaware. He beat
> 'Gainst his barred sides his speckled wings, and made
> A sound like distant thunder."

In the same way the melodious bobolink of our Northern pastures, when it emigrates to the South, grows fat, and is highly estimated by epicures under the name of the reed-bird. Still farther South he is known as the rice-bird, and in Jamaica as the butter-bird. This contains a moral. The poet who grows fat and prosperous loses his song and is doomed.

The bird called in England the yellow "hammer" is the yellow-bunting; but it should properly be the yellow-ammer, like the German *ammer*, a bunting. In some parts of the United States the name is applied to the flicker or golden-winged woodpecker. The hedge-sparrow is not a real sparrow. Its correct name is hedge accentor, and it is closely related to the robins and redstarts. Dr. Bowdler-Sharpe, in his "Natural History Museum," says, "In all other respects, except that of the similarity of coloring of the upper surface, it is quite different from the sparrow, and as regards voice, nesting habits, color of eggs, etc., it has nothing in common with the latter bird." The so-called muscovy duck has no claim on Russia; it is only the musk duck with a longer name. Nuttall's "Ornithology" says: "The term muscovy is wholly misapplied, since it is an exclusive native of the warmer and tropical parts of America and its islands." The night-jar is often called the "goat-sucker," from the notion formerly in vogue and not even yet quite extinct, that he had the habit of sucking the teats of wild goats, cows, and sheep. At evening he hovers close by the udders of cattle and goats as they lie stretched in the meadows; but he is not milking them — he comes as a friend. The night-jar snaps up the flies that annoy the animals, while the cattle never whisk their tails so long as the bird attends them.

The Sparrow of the Bible. —

"Are not two sparrows sold for a farthing?" — Matt. x., 29.

"I am as a sparrow alone upon the house-top." — Psalm CII., 7.

The bird here mentioned is not the common English sparrow, which is unknown in the Holy Land, though tree-sparrows are abundant. The psalmist probably alluded to a species of thrush frequently seen perched on the villagers' houses in Judea. It is a bird usually *alone*, and rarely more than a pair are seen together. In the forty allusions in the Old Testament all but two are rendered indifferently "bird" or "fowl."

Birds lose their Way. — Many imagine that the annual arrival of our migratory birds is because they "know their way by inherited impulse;" that they come and go "with certainty." If they read Dixon's "The Migration of Birds," they will find that birds blunder and lose their way; that they gradually learn the various landmarks on the road; that they almost invariably lose their way in darkness or fog; that, in fact, "the mysterious sense of direction" is a myth. It is now the theory that birds go in waves. Our robins, for instance, may migrate to Florida; while those from Labrador or farther north winter here, giving rise to the notion that some of our robins stay with us all the year round.

Do Birds die of Cold? — It was reported in the

newspapers that after the great frost that destroyed so many orange plantations in the South in 1895 the coast was lined with the bodies of bluebirds and other birds that had perished of the cold. On Feb. 16, 1895, the London " Echo " said : " Vast numbers of song birds have fallen a prey to the *cold*." But a writer in the February number of the " Cornhill " says : " I have never known a bird in this country or in North America during the terribly severe winter of 1875–76 die of cold, but I have seen hundreds and thousands of birds dying and dead of starvation. . . . No wind direct from the North pole, over trackless and snow-mantled Greenland or Iceland, ever ruffled the equanimity of a pigeon on the farthest point of Scotland if it were not pinched for food and water.

" I have watched my pigeons during biting hurricanes, perched on the highest ridge of their house, preening their feathers, and literally cooing in the blast with delight. Nor do pigeons, like human beings, grow more sensitive to cold as they advance in years.

" Birds, I believe, never absolutely die of cold. I question if they ever feel it as man does, and I attribute their invulnerability to the closeness and warmth of their feathery covering, the peculiar texture of the skin of their feet and legs, the fatty plumpness of their flesh, the warmth and richness of their blood, and other purely physiological characteristics."

Mr. Thomson, the head keeper of the Zoölogical Society's Gardens, is reported as saying that no birds have died from cold alone at the Zoo, even during the terribly severe winter of '94 and '95, and he instances the fact that many birds, as the ivory gull, spend not only the summer, but the entire winter, within the arctic circle.

How Birds sleep. — Most children believe that birds sleep with their heads under their wings. The well-known nursery rhyme says:

> " The north wind doth blow,
>   And we shall have snow ;
> What will the robin do then, poor thing ?
>   He'll go to the barn
>   And keep himself warm,
> And put his head under his wing, poor thing."

R. H. Dana says, in " Two Years before the Mast":

" One of the finest sights that I have ever seen was an albatross asleep upon the water, during a calm off Cape Horn, when a heavy sea was running. There being no breeze, the surface of the water was unbroken, but a long heavy swell was running, and we saw the fellow, all white, directly ahead of us, asleep upon the waves, with his head under his wing."

Literature is full of allusions to birds sleeping in that way, and illustrations in many books give the same impression. Indeed, a casual glance at a sleeping bird appears to confirm it, but no bird in the world sleeps in that way. Most birds turn their heads round and lay them along their backs, nestling them well down into their feathers, so that they are almost, if not quite, concealed. The truth of this assertion is confirmed by the famous authority on bird structure, Dr. Bowdler Sharpe, and also the late Mr. Clarence Bartlett, by whom the habits of hundreds of birds have been personally noted, night and day, at the London Zoo.

The Eagle. — This bird does not fly downward beak first; it never does this except in pictures: it always comes down feet first. Mackerel gulls and other divers plunge head first into the water, making scarcely any splash.

The Ibis that is not Sacred. — The scarlet ibis is not the sacred ibis. The bird that the Egyptians worshipped is black and white.

The Owl's Toes. — Illustrations in most non-technical books treating of owls always show three toes directed forward; but the owl perches with only two toes visible, except occasionally when on a wide surface, and then the fourth toe, which is reversible, may be brought half-way toward the front if the bird so will.

The Nightingale. — It is a delusion to suppose that the song of this bird is heard only by night, for though it usually sings after sunset, it may be sometimes heard in full song throughout the day. One variety of nightingale sings in the day only.

Truly the name, from *nihtegale*, indicates a bird that sings by night. Another common mistake is that he modestly shuns the haunts of men. He is often heard singing unabashed within a few yards of a noisy road, and with people watching him.

The Turkey not from Turkey. — Johnson's Dictionary defines turkey as "a large domestic fowl supposed to be brought from Turkey."

The Spaniards found them in immense flocks, and introduced them into Europe after the conquest of Mexico in 1518. It is supposed that the Portuguese, who called them peru, not pavo, a peacock, imported them from Spain to Bombay, whence they came to Italy and were called in Italian and French "Indian fowl." And it is believed that they were introduced into England and Germany from Constantinople. Shakespeare and Bacon both mention the turkey-cock.

Ostriches and their Feathers. — It is often asserted that the removal of feathers from the ostrich is a painful operation, because they are pulled out. This is not true. The universal practice during the last twenty years is to cut the feather about two inches above the socket. The stumps are then allowed to remain in the bird for two months, by which time they become loose and are painlessly withdrawn. The story that the ostrich hides its head in the sand when pursued, thinking that no one can see it as it cannot see itself, has no basis in fact.

The Flamingo. — The "Boys' Own Natural History," by Wood, published in 1897, says: "The nest of the flamingo is a *tall, conical* structure of *mud.* . . . When the bird sits on the nest her feet rest on the ground, or *hang* into the water." It is generally depicted sitting *à cheval*, with one long leg hanging down each side of a high cone-shaped nest. But in real life its nest is nothing more than a *low* pile of weeds and leaves cemented with marl in shallow water, and the bird sits on its eggs like any other bird, and manages to *fold* its legs under itself. The name is derived from its color, not because it is the Flemish bird, as some suppose.

Hawks and Blackbirds. — Farmers kill hawks and blackbirds as marauders. The Department of Agriculture has shown conclusively that out of seventy-three species of hawks and owls in the United States only five were injurious to vegetation. They feed mainly on mice and noxious insects.

The chicken-hawk or red-tailed hawk rarely carries off a chicken. For every chicken it destroys it is estimated to eat fifty mice, and from a thousand to two thousand grasshoppers. Yet the legislatures of our States often offer bounties for hawk scalps, and thus directly pay for the destruction of other birds no less valuable. By the way, the common contemptuous expression "he does not know a hawk from a handsaw" (see "Hamlet" II., 2) is shown by Mr. Skeat to be a curious misappropriation of terms: handsaw should be hernshaw, a young heron. But the word hawker has nothing to do with hawks; it comes from the old English huck, to peddle; huckster.

Moths. — The idea that moths eat holes in our curtains and clothes is wrong. They eat nothing, and the mischief attributed to them is done after they are dead, their death happening as soon as they have laid their eggs. And they are not averse to laying them in camphor or lavender bags, cedar closets, or where the ill-smelling moth ball pervades the air. To the maggots from these eggs should be attached the blame for the actual devastation.

The Lady-bird. — The lady-bird is not a bird, but a beetle. The dictionary states that it feeds on plant lice. This is a mistake. Its grub, which makes its appearance some four or five weeks after the lady-bird has settled on a plant, does all the feeding. It resembles a tiny crocodile both in voracity and shape, and will suck dry hundreds of " blight " spots in a few hours.

The House-fly. — The house-fly has no suckers in its feet, as some imagine, but is provided with moist, hairy pads which can stick to any smooth surface. For rough surfaces each foot is provided with a pair of hooks.

Blunders about Bees. — In Shakespeare's second play of " Henry IV.," IV., 4, the king says: " Like the bee . . . our thighs packed with wax, our mouths with honey." But bees carry their wax

in their "tails" and honey in their stomachs.
Elsewhere we are told that when "the old bees
die, the young possess their hive." But there are
no successive generations of bees; they are all the
offspring of the same mother, and possess the hive
by mutual arrangement, and not by heredity; when
it gets too full the superfluous bees go off with a
queen bee to the "colonies," leaving the old folks
at home, as it were. Another error regarding the
bee is that it uses its sting only to avenge an injury
or in self-defence. On the contrary, the acid serves
as a preservation of the honey. Not only is it used
in minute portions throughout the entire process of
manufacture, but it is also employed, and much
more freely, to complete the cells, and cover them
with the tiny cap. Humble bees are not so called
because they are humble or inferior to the honey
bee, but because they *hum!*

Locusts are Good to Eat. — John the Baptist's
food was locusts and wild honey. The Greek word
is *akris*, plural *akrides*, and it does not signify the
bean-pods of the locust-tree as some ignorant com-
mentators affirm, but the insect. It has been eaten
in many places in Asia and Africa from early times.
The Bedouins string them together, and eat them
on their journeys with unleavened cake and butter.
Bushmen esteem them their greatest luxury. Dr.
Livingstone speaks highly of the same kind of food,
declaring it to be superior to shrimps, and Mr. J.
T. Bent, in "The Ruined Cities of Mashonaland,"

1895, says he found Mashonas and Matabele busily engaged in cooking locusts. Honey is eaten with locusts whenever it can be obtained. On the other hand, honey would be quite unnecessary with the locust-bean, which is itself sufficiently sweet. It is worthy of note that the locust and grasshopper were not prohibited to the Jews (see Leviticus xi., 22).

Why the Scorpion stings Itself.—It is not true that scorpions, unable to escape from fire, deliberately commit suicide by stinging themselves. Experiments show that the scorpion's poison has no effect on itself, and that when placed in a test-tube, so that the sting cannot be used, and then subjected to a moderate heat (50 deg. C.) it quickly dies. When the solar rays are directed upon it by a lens, it raises its tail and tries to strike the cause of irritation, and when it dies it is alleged to have committed suicide; but it has really been killed by the heat to which it was exposed. Scorpions have been seen to sting themselves in the case of local irritation, if, for instance, acids, mustard, or the like be applied. Not succeeding in ridding itself of the annoyance by ordinary means, the creature directs its sting on the point afflicted, with the intention, not of killing itself, but rather of destroying the cause of pain; in this case it does not die.

The Nautilus does not sail.—

> "This is the ship of pearl, which, poets feign,
> Sails the unshadowed main,"

says Dr. Oliver Wendell Holmes. Pope advises:

"Learn of the little nautilus to sail,
Spread the thin oar and catch the driving gale."

Webster's dictionary says it is "a kind of shell-fish furnished with a membrane that [which] serves it as a sail." Thus is perpetuated the fable that the nautilus floats on the surface of the sea with concave side of its shell upward, and that it holds out some of its arms after the manner of sails to catch the breeze, and directs its course with the remainder by using them as oars. Aristotle believed this, and it has been a favorite simile for poets ever since; but naturalists know that the hard-shelled nautilus and the thin-shelled argonaut float through, not on, the water, that the arms are packed together in a straight line to serve for a rudder, and that a stream of water underneath drives them along. And when these shell-fish crawl along the bottom, the so-called boat is inverted like the shell of a snail.

As Merry as a Grig. — "Merry as a grig" is a common comparison. Grig is a cricket; but though the cricket is the emblem of cheerful content, the term in the comparison should probably be "As merry as a Greek," the Greeks being notorious for their happy natures.

Slow-worms and Glow-worms. — The blind worm, or slow-worm, anatomically considered, is not a snake, but a lizard without visible legs; it is any-thing but blind, in spite of its name, and its eyes, though small, are brilliant. That it is a lizard is proved by the presence of rudimentary legs beneath the skin; the eyes are furnished with movable lids — an arrangement not belonging to snakes, but found in lizards; the tongue is notched at the point, but not forked as with snakes; finally, the expansion of the jaws and the shape of the scales are quite different from the snake's. The idea that this little snakelike lizard is venomous is also erroneous. In calling it a worm we retain the original meaning of the name; the old English for any snake or dragon is *wyrm* — that is, worm. On the other hand, the glow-worm is not a worm, nor has it the slightest resemblance to one, but is most emphatically a beetle; the coral anemone is incorrectly called the coral "insect."

Snakes do not coil round a Tree. — We often see snakes represented by artists and in stuffed specimens in museums as coiling their bodies around trunks and branches in close, corkscrew-like coils. A live snake never does this. It simply glides up with the whole body extended in a straight line, gripping with the tips of its expanded ribs, and clinging with the concave rows of pointed scales as it presses against the bark; and after reaching a branch it maintains its position by still clinging, neither round it nor half round it, but along its upper surface. The tail alone is prehensile, and is used particularly when the snake wishes to hang down or to reach over to another branch.

Snakes have Ears. — "Deaf as an adder" is a popular comparison. Many persons imagine that the auditory apparatus is either wanting or present in a merely rudimentary state in snakes. This, however, is all wrong. Cornish, in his "Life at the Zoo," says: "At the first note of a violin the cobra instantly raised its head and fixed its bright yellow eyes with a set gaze on the little door at the back." Snakes generally rustle away at the sound of footsteps. There is no reason to suppose that deafness is more prevalent among snakes than among creatures with more prominent ears.

Concerning Rattlesnakes. — Many think the rattlesnake rattles only when it is bent on attacking. But Darwin thinks it probable that the purpose of the rattling, like that of the cobra in distending its hood, is to alarm birds which attack even the most venomous snakes. Others imagine that a rattlesnake is a magnanimous enemy, and gives a sort of warning by rattling before it strikes; but it very frequently strikes horses without the least note of warning. Another picturesque error regarding the rattlesnake is that when it is about to fight it coils itself up like a watchspring, in order to leap forward at an object some distance ahead. It simply gathers itself into a number of folds resembling a pile of S's, and darts out but three-fourths of its own length, and very rarely accomplishes even that in actual warfare.

How Deep-sea Fish fall up. — When a man ascends to a very high altitude, his blood, relieved from a portion of the atmospheric pressure, forces

its way out through the nose, ears, eyes, and
mouth. If he could go higher still, his whole
body would expand and fall to pieces. So it is
with creatures inhabiting the depths of the ocean.
At three miles below the surface their bodies are
subject internally (by gases) and externally to a
pressure of more than two tons to the square inch,
and under this pressure are solid enough, and also,
because this pressure does not increase their density, are comfortable enough. When brought to
the surface in dredges the bodies of such creatures
are of the consistency of pulp, even their bones
become loose in texture, their eyes — when they
have any — start out of their heads, and often their
bodies burst asunder. Hickson, in his " Fauna
of the Deep Sea," says : " The fish which [that] live
in the enormous depths are liable to a curious form
of accident. If, in chasing their prey, or for any
other reason, they rise to a considerable distance
above the floor of the ocean, the gases of their
swimming bladders become greatly expanded, and
their specific gravity [becomes] greatly reduced. If
the muscles are not strong enough to drive the
body downwards, the fish, becoming more and more
distended as it goes, is killed on its long and involuntary journey to the surface of the sea. The deep-
sea fish, then, are exposed to a danger that no
other creatures in this world are subject to, namely,
that of tumbling upwards."

CHAPTER VI.

COMMON MISTAKES OF MANY KINDS.

Ancient Statues were colored and adorned with Real Trappings. — Plaster casts in museums do not correctly represent the ancient Greek and Roman marble statues. The originals were often painted in gorgeous colors, and gilded, and covered with ornaments. The Greeks and the Romans were much fonder of bright hues than we are. The color covered the entire surface of the marble, both nude parts and draperies. In recent times experiments have been made by many sculptors and painters in coloring statuary, but it is repugnant to modern taste. Professor Lanciani, speaking upon the universality of the practice of coloring marble statues in ancient times, says of the Roman statues found in Rome: "In good condition, in pure earth and at a considerable depth, one-half showed traces of colors at the very moment they were brought to light. Of this half two-thirds lost their polychromy at once, and one-third still preserve it."

There can be no doubt, either, that metal, cord, wooden, and leather accessories were affixed to the marble. This is evident from the cylindrical holes in some of the Parthenon sculptures in the British

Museum. The bridles and reins were real, the sandal-straps were of leather, the stone hands[1] grasped actual weapons, and there are unmistakable examples in frieze carving that the cattle led to sacrifice struggled against straps or cords.

Why the Cock stands on Steeples. —The common practice of setting a cock on a church steeple is popularly associated with the reproach that bird once conveyed to St. Peter. But in very early times the cock placed on the tops of sacred trees and turned by the wind was believed to disperse evil spirits and ward off approaching calamities: its living prototype did the same by its crowing. The cock still stand on may-poles in North Germany.

Minerva's Ægis. — The Ægis borne by Zeus or Athene is frequently taken to be an ordinary shield. Originally it was a simple goat-skin (as the original of the word proves) used to support the shield and at the same time to serve as a protection and covering. Thus it came to be confused by the ancients themselves with the shield or with the breast-plate. It really was a breast-covering or kind of short cloak, set with the Gorgon's head and fringed with snakes.

Pan a Purifier. — The Greek god Pan which modern poets affect to worship is commonly con-

---

[1] " Rings. Ancient Roman. Diameter of bezel, 2⅛ inches. Ring for a colossal statue." (Copy of label at South Kensington Museum.)

nected with the word *pan*, meaning all, as in pantheism. It really comes from the Sanskrit Pavana (from the root *pû*, to purify), the wind-god.

Prometheus and Fire. — The legend that connected Prometheus with the generous gift of fire arose from the Sanskrit, in which Pramantha is the fire drill; it has really nothing to do etymologically with forethought.

Venus was not a Well-formed Woman. — The so-called Venus di Medici is generally regarded as a " perfect type of perfect womanhood." Professor Chadwick thinks that she is not worthy of being either a physiological or psychological standard. He points out that the narrow chest indicates weak lungs, that the shoulders are not well braced up, that the cranium and face show no trace of mental vigor, that her limbs show want of muscular training, and that, as a type of what a mother and mistress of a home should be, she is contemptible.

Pipe-coloring not Modern. — We are apt to think that, because tobacco is used in pipes, the art of pipe-coloring dates only from the discovery by Columbus of the Island of Tobago, or from the time of the importation of tobacco by Sir Walter Raleigh. But it is well known that smoking of various leaves — sweet fern and perhaps Indian hemp and opium — was regarded as a luxury even in prehistoric times. Dr. Petrie says that bronze smoking-pipes are frequently found in our Irish tumuli, or sepulchral mounds, of the most remote antiquity. "On the monument of Donough O'Brien, King of Thomond, who was killed in 1267, and interred in the Abbey of Corcumrac in the county of Clare, he is represented in the usual recumbent posture, with the short pipe or dhudeen in his mouth." It is said that in the mortar of the Kirkstall Abbey Church, which was built in the twelfth century and fell in ruins in 1779, several small smoking-pipes were found.

In Asia and Africa, as well as in America, the pipe was known in prehistoric times, and in Europe generally it has been in use since and during the Roman period, if not before.

Wear your Furs outside. — According to the poem the Indian woman, Nokomis, when she made a pair of mittens,

> " Put the skin-side inside outside,
> Put the fur-side outside inside,"

and many persons imagine that it would be an advantage to wear the fur of garments and muffs inside instead of out. Actual tests, however, have proved that furs conserve far greater heat on the body when the hair *is exposed* to the air than when the leather is.

Is Death Painless? — Dr. Roberts Bartholow, formerly Dean of Jefferson Medical College, declared that he had seen persons die in all manner of ways, and he firmly believed that dissolution itself was not only painless, but in most cases blissful.

Even where features are distorted it is by involuntary muscular contraction, and usually where suffering has preceded death the features take on a pleased expression as if the body were at perfect rest. Freezing to death is generally imagined to be the least painful of deaths, but the great Russian painter, Vasili Verestchagin, says of the prisoner defenders of Plevna, who fell by ones and twos in the road through the forest: "I closely examined the faces of the corpses lying in every imaginable position along the road, and convinced myself that every face bore the impress of deep suffering."

When Death is Most Busy.—Opinion has it that the largest number of deaths occur in the early morning hours, while dwellers by the sea are rather generally credited with the belief that the dying most frequently "go out with the tide." Careful observations made in hospitals are said to have shown that death takes place with fairly equal frequency during the twenty-four hours of the day. An inquiry lately made in Paris showed that death is just a little less busy between seven and eleven o'clock in the evening, but that with this exception the proportion was about even. The death-rate among dwellers in apartment houses is said to be noticeably larger on the third and fourth floors. This is perhaps due to the extra exertion put on the heart by the effort in mounting the steep stairs.

A Popular Mistake about the Heart.—The heart is not situated on the *left* side of the thorax, but in the *centre* immediately behind the breast bone and between the lungs; only the point is directed toward the left side, and if a line be drawn down the centre of the chest to divide the heart into two portions, the rather larger portion will be found on the right side. Physiologically, the heart is nothing but a powerful automatic muscle. In the language of love, it is the seat of the affections; but the ancients attributed that supremacy to the liver.

Surgeons say that when a bullet enters the brain the action of the heart is, for the moment, actually stimulated, not depressed, but that the respiration is stopped, and the proper treatment, as in the case of a half-drowned person, is artificial respiration.

The heart is a force-pump measuring six by four inches; it beats seventy times a minute, 36,792,000 times a year, and in three score and ten years 2,575,440,000 times, forcing $2\frac{1}{2}$ ounces of blood each time, or 7.03 tons a day; 30 pounds of blood goes through every three minutes, equalling 122 tons raised 1 foot. In seventy years this little organ raises 178,830 tons of blood. In each drop of blood there are 1,000,000 corpuscles; 20,000,000 are destroyed at each inhalation.

Bullets that act like Explosives. — In the recent war with Spain the charge was made that the Spaniards were firing explosive bullets at our men. The small Mauser balls made clean wounds, and when they did not instantly kill often went through the lungs or the brain, disabling their victim, but leaving him easily cured. But other bullets made such ugly wounds that it was thought they must have been filled, contrary to the courtesy of nations, with bursting materials. In reality, the appearance of explosion arises from the nature of the substance penetrated. In yielding flesh the impulse of a large bullet is distributed laterally in all directions, and the wound is correspondingly torn. By firing into wet dough every indication of an explosion is made, while similar bullets directed at solid substances, like bone, have made only round holes.

Comets and Collisions. — Nervous persons are afraid the earth may be struck by a comet. According to Babinet the chance of a collision between our earth and a comet will occur once in fifteen million years. Arago said there was one chance out of 281,000,000.

Round-robins. — Some ingenious though perverse etymologists have tried to derive the expression round-robin from the French *rond ruban*. But no Frenchman ever heard of such an expression. It is mistakenly supposed to have been first used in 1659 by sailors to call attention to existing evils, and to have been devised so that the signatures should be equally prominent, that, paradoxically speaking, there should seem to be no ringleader. But a round-robin was presented to Parliament in 1643. An English writer sensibly believes that, like the word " Jack," Robin, the double diminutive of Robert, was " a picturesque and euphonious sub-

stitute for 'thing' or 'object.'" Applied to a pan-
cake, it is at least two hundred and fifty years old.

Plump Children. — Appearances are deceitful.
A plump child is not necessarily a healthy child.
Dr. E. Smith, in a work on foods, says: "The addition of sugar to fresh cow's milk greatly lessens its
nutritive value, and induces a tendency to muscular
starvation." And he concludes: "The more fatten-
ing infants' foods are, the less likely they are to
make muscular men and women."

The London "Lancet" declares that fat children
are not only backward in learning to walk, but are
also less able to resist disease; they are the quickest
to succumb to measles, diarrhœa, whooping-cough,
and bronchitis.

There is no Nourishment in Beef-tea. — Beef-
tea is a stimulant and not a food. Dr. Geo. Her-
schel is authority for saying there is no nourishment in beef-tea at all. It is *absolutely poisonous
(in large doses) to those engaged in active exercise,*
as the extractives which it contains in such quantities are analogous in composition and action to the
poisons that accumulate in the muscle during exercise, and cause the sensation of fatigue. Further.
the potash salts in beef-tea act as direct depressing
agents to the heart. Moreover, as ordinarily made,
it consists of the flavoring agents (extractive) and
salts of the meat, together with a certain quantity
of gelatine. The strong beef-tea, made in a covered jar in the oven, on cooling sets into a thick

jelly, which is gelatine. This thick, strong, gluey beef-tea is not digestible, for the digestion of gelatine is a complicated process. Moreover, gelatine, being a proximate organic principle, is incapable alone of sustaining life.

It is supposed that a large proportion of the nourishing part of the meat is extracted, and that the remainder from which beef-tea has been made is of no food value. This is entirely erroneous, as the proteid, or nourishing part of meat, is insoluble in boiling water, or, in fact, in water above 160° Fahr. In such beef-tea all the real meat is thrown away in the *débris* remaining in the jar after the tea has been strained off. This fact can easily be proved by feeding two dogs, the one on the strongest beef-tea that can be made, and the other on the shreds of meat from which it has been extracted. The former will soon die of starvation: the other will live in perfect health and strength. On the other hand, the lean-meat diet has also its dangers. While it develops the strength, it overtaxes the poison-eliminating functions of the liver.

Trust not Filtered Water. — To filter water does not purify it from anything *dissolved* in it, but only from particles *floating* in it. If tea, or brandy and water, are poured through a charcoal filter, they are still brandy and water, or tea. Hence water in which sewage has been dissolved is not purified by filtration ; for though the water lose its bad smell and any foreign matter it may suspend, there is no alteration in its composition. The report of the Medical Commission at the instance of the "British Medical Journal" (1895) condemned filtration as affording no protection against choleric, typhoid, and other germs. The inquiry was based on experiments with twenty-four kinds of table filters in general use, and points out that what is usually called "pure water" in this connection should be called "clear water" or "palatable," as without the precaution of previous boiling it may be, bacteriologically, unwholesome water. Of course these remarks are probably inapplicable to improvements in filtration such as the Pasteur-Chamberland process.

Mistaken Notions about the Sea.—Story writers dealing with the wonders of the deep have imagined that dead bodies, cargoes of ships, and ships themselves sink down only part way, the density of the water keeping them from reaching the bottom. But as such bodies are of greater density than water, they *must* sink to the very bottom; though the pressure of the water increases in proportion to its depth, its density, even under the greatest pressure, is but slightly increased, and never sufficiently to make it identical with the density of any falling body — the only condition in which suspension could occur. The sea in order to move heavy bodies like rocks has to overcome only about half of the weight of the object. A solid body immersed becomes lighter by the weight of water which it displaces.

The First Transatlantic Steamer. — Some cyclopædias say that the first vessel to cross the Atlantic by steam was the "Rising Sun" in 1818; others say the first steam voyage was made across the Atlantic by the "Savannah." All are wrong. A tablet has lately been erected in the Great Hall of the Parliament Buildings, Ottawa, commemorating the fact that the first vessel to cross the Atlantic propelled entirely by steam was the "Royal William," built in Canada in 1833 by James Groudie. Some fourteen years previously the "Savannah" crossed from Savannah to London, but the wood that she carried for fuel ran short, and she was compelled to cover the greater part of the distance with the aid of sails. And the claim of the "Rising Sun" has yet to be proved. The "Savannah" was a full-rigged ship of 380 tons, with a pair of paddle wheels so constructed that in a storm they could be unshipped. On her first voyage she was chased a whole day off the coast of Ireland by a revenue cruiser, which took her for a ship on fire. Lombroso says, "Blasco de Garay seems to have propelled a vessel by steam and paddles in the harbor of Barcelona in 1543."

Steam Locomotion. — Stephenson was not the first man to construct a steam railway. The father of the locomotive was Richard Trevithick, of Cornwall, England. On Feb. 24, 1804, his tramway engine conveyed a load of ten tons of bar iron and seventy passengers nine miles to Merthyr Tydvil; but though it worked satisfactorily, it was regarded as more expensive than horses.

The same year Oliver Evans made a machine called Eructor Amphibolis, for dredging purposes. It was mounted on a scow with four wheels, and after going, self-impelled by its own steam, from his shop in Philadelphia to the Schuylkill, it entered the river, and by means of a paddle-wheel proceeded round to the Delaware and performed its work of dredging.

The first engine to carry passengers on a track in the United States was designed by Colonel John Stevens, of Hoboken. It had a cog-wheel that fitted into a cast-iron rack in the centre of the track. It had four wooden wheels, the tires without flanges. This was in 1825, the same year that George Stephenson's engine "Locomotion" ran successfully between Stockton and Darlington.

It is a very pretty legend that when Napoleon was bound for St. Helena on the "Bellerophon," he saw a ship passing by under steam and bearing the name of Fulton, who, according to the story, had proposed to him to move vessels by steam and found no favorable response. Indeed, Bonaparte is said to have called him hard names. Neither did Dionys Papin escape from the anger of the Landgrave Karl of Hesse by fleeing on a steamboat of his invention. He experimented in steamboats in the seventeenth century on the Fulda, but unsuccessfully. Blasco de Garay proposed in 1540 to make ships move without oars or sail, and in 1543 successfully propelled a ship according to his promise. Karl did not call him a fool and swindler, as Napoleon called Fulton, but though he saw no good in the machine gave him 200,000 maravedis and paid the expenses. Before Fulton, Branca 1629, Savary 1698, Hull in 1736, Newcomb Watt, Perrier Murdock, in 1775, Jouffroy in 1781, and others, made more or less successful experiments with steam as a motor for navigation.

The Freezing Power of Water. — If water is kept quite still its temperature may be reduced to much below 32° without solidifying; in fact, it is possible to bring it actually below zero in a liquid state, but the instant the least motion occurs it solidifies in a mass. The adoption of 32° for ordinary purposes is based on experiments with *pure* water in a greater or less state of agitation at the level of the mean tide at Liverpool. Water when it freezes expands, and the leaking of water pipes after a thaw signifies that the ice had acted as a plug till it began to melt. The mischief was done at the moment of solidification.

Primary Colors. — The artist's primary colors are yellow, red, and blue, because he finds that neither of these colors can be formed by the mixture of others; on the other hand, the physicist, who deals with colored rays of light, shows that yellow can be formed by mixing red and green rays, and hence is not a primary color; while violet, which cannot be obtained by any admixture, he considers to be one of the three primaries.

There is no National Holiday. — Not even the Fourth of July is a national holiday. Congress has at various times appointed special holidays. In the second session of the Fifty-third Congress it passed an act making Labor Day a public holiday in the District of Columbia, and it has recognized the existence of certain days as holidays, for commercial purposes, in such legislation as the Bankruptcy Act; but with the exception named there is no general statute on the subject. The proclamation of the President designating a day of Thanksgiving makes it a holiday in only those States that provide for it by law.

The following is a list of the legal holidays in the various States:

January 1. New Year's Day: In all the States except Massachusetts, New Hampshire, and Rhode Island.

January 8. Anniversary of the Battle of New Orleans: In Louisiana.

January 19. Lee's Birthday: In Georgia, North Carolina, and Virginia.

February 12. Lincoln's Birthday: In Illinois.

February 22. Washington's Birthday: In all the States except Arkansas, Iowa, and Mississippi.

March 2. Anniversary of Texan Independence : In Texas.

March 4. Firemen's Anniversary : In New Orleans, La.

April 1, 1896. State Election Day : In Rhode Island.

April 3, 1896. Good Friday : In Alabama, Louisiana, Maryland, Pennsylvania, and Tennessee.

April 19. Patriots' Day : In Massachusetts.

April 21. Anniversary of the Battle of San Jacinto : In Texas.

April 26. Memorial Day : In Alabama and Georgia.

May 10. Memorial Day : In North Carolina.

May 20. Anniversary of the Signing of the Mecklenburg Declaration of Independence : In North Carolina.

May 30. Decoration Day : In Arizona, California, Colorado, Connecticut, Delaware, District of Columbia, Iowa, Illinois, Indiana, Kansas, Maine, Maryland, Massachusetts, Michigan, Minnesota, Montana, Nebraska, Nevada, New Hampshire, New Jersey, New York, North Dakota, Ohio, Oklahoma, Oregon, Pennsylvania, Rhode Island, Tennessee, Utah, Vermont, Wisconsin, Washington, and Wyoming.

June 3. Jefferson Davis's Birthday : In Florida.

July 4. Independence Day : In all the States.

July 24. Pioneers' Day : In Utah.

First Monday in September. Labor Day : In

Alabama, California, Colorado, Connecticut, Delaware, Florida, Georgia, Illinois, Indiana, Iowa, Kansas, Maine, Maryland, Massachusetts, Michigan, Montana, Nebraska, New Hampshire, New Jersey, New York, Ohio, Oregon, Pennsylvania, South Carolina, South Dakota, Tennessee, Texas, Utah, Virginia, Washington.

September 9. Admission Day: In California.

October 31. Admission Day: In Nevada.

November. General Election Day: In Arizona, California, Idaho, Indiana, Kansas, Maryland, Minnesota, Missouri, Montana, Nevada, New Hampshire, New Jersey, New York, North Dakota, Ohio, Pennsylvania, South Carolina, South Dakota, Tennessee, Texas, West Virginia, Washington, Wisconsin, and Wyoming.

November. Thanksgiving Day: This is observed in all the States, though in some it is not a statutory holiday.

December 25. Christmas Day: In all the States, and in South Carolina the two succeeding days in addition.

Sundays and Fast Days are legal holidays in all the States that designate them as such.

Arbor Day is a legal holiday in Kansas, North Dakota, Rhode Island, and Wyoming, the day being set by the Governor; in Nebraska, April 22; California, September 9; Colorado, on the third Friday in April; Montana, third Tuesday in April; Utah, first Saturday in April; and Idaho, on Friday after May 1.

Every Saturday after 12 o'clock noon is a legal holiday in New York, New Jersey, and the city of New Orleans, Pennsylvania and Maryland, and June 1 to September 30 in New Castle County, Delaware.

Is Friday an Unlucky Day?—The belief is widespread that Friday is an unlucky day. Why should it be? One reason given is that Christ was crucified on Friday. Perhaps it arises from the popular notion that Friday is a changeable day, or, as Chaucer calls it, *gerful*. He says:

> " Selde is the Friday al the wyke alyke."

An old Shropshire couplet says:

> " Friday's a day as'll have his trick;
> The fairest or foulest day of the wick."

As a proof of the universality of the superstition among all nations and ranks, it is curious to note that the shipping returns of all countries show a much lower sailing rate on Friday than any other day of the week.

And yet Friday is really the luckiest day in the week! It is Frea, day of the god of peace and joy and fruitfulness, whose emblems, borne aloft by dancing maidens, brought increase to every field and stall they visited. Friday is the Muhammedan Sabbath, called *el Jum'â*, " the assembly."

Here is a partial list of fortunate Fridays that might well dispel forever the absurd notion:

On Friday, Aug. 21, 1492, Christopher Columbus first sailed upon his great voyage of discovery from Palos, in Spain. On the 11th day of September, which happened upon a Friday, while in mid-ocean, to the consternation of his officers and men, the needle of the compass fluctuated and fell off in an unexplainable manner, and it was then ´that all but Columbus lost faith in the enterprise. It was on Friday, Oct. 12, 1492, that Columbus first discovered land. On Friday, Jan. 4, 1493, he sailed on his return to Spain, where he landed in safety on a Friday. On Friday, Nov. 22, 1493, he arrived at Hispaniola, on his second voyage to America. It was on Friday, June 13, 1494, that he discovered the continent of America.

On Friday, March 5, 1496, Henry VIII., of England, gave John Cabot his commission which led to his discovery of North America. This is the first American state paper in England.

Friday, Sept. 7, 1505, Melendez founded St. Augustine, the oldest town in the United States.

Friday, Nov. 10, 1620, the " Mayflower," with the Pilgrims, made the harbor of Provincetown, and on the same day signed the august compact, the forerunner of our present Constitution. On Friday, Dec. 22, 1620, the Pilgrims made their final landing on Plymouth Rock.

George Washington was born on Friday, Feb. 22, 1732, in Westmoreland County, Va., near the banks of the Potomac River.

Bunker Hill was seized and fortified on Friday, June 16, 1776.

Friday, Oct. 7, 1777, the surrender of Saratoga was made, which had such power and influence in inducing France to declare herself in favor of our cause.

Friday, Sept. 22, 1780, Arnold's treason was laid bare, which saved us and our country from destruction.

The surrender of Yorktown, the crowning glory of the American army, occurred on Friday, Oct. 19, 1781.

Friday, July 7, 1776, the motion was made in Congress, by John Adams, and seconded by Richard Henry Lee, that the United Colonies were, and of right ought to be, free and independent.

The first Masonic Lodge in America was organized on Friday, Nov. 21, 1721.

Bismarck, Gladstone, and Disraeli were born on Friday.

Friday, April 8, 1646, the first known newspaper advertisement was published in the "Imperial Intelligencer," in England.

Friday, July 1, 1825, General Lafayette was welcomed to Boston and feasted by the Freemasons and citizens, and attended at the laying of the corner-stone, at Bunker's Hill, of the monument erected to perpetuate the remembrance of the defenders of the rights and liberties of America.

The Hudson River was discovered on Friday, March 25, 1609.

On Friday, March 18, 1776, the "stamp act" was repealed in England.

On Friday, Nov. 28, 1814, the first newspaper ever printed by steam, the London "Times," was printed.

On Friday, Jan. 13, 1785, Gen. Winfield Scott was born in Dinwiddie County, Va.

Friday, May 14, 1586, Gabriel Farenheit, usually regarded as the inventor of the common mercurial thermometer, was born.

Friday, Dec. 25, 1742, Sir Isaac Newton, the illustrious philosopher, was born.

Martin Luther was born on Friday, Nov. 10, 1543, at Eiseben, in the county of Mansfield, in Upper Saxony.

Friday, June 3, the steam vessel "Savannah" sailed from Savannah to Liverpool.

George Stephenson, the father of railways, was born on Friday.

The "Great Eastern" left the Irish coast to lay the Atlantic cable on Friday, and reached Heart's Content on Friday.

Queen Victoria was married on a Friday.

The battle of Waterloo was fought, the Bastile was destroyed, Moscow was burned, and the battle of New Orleans was fought on Friday.

On Friday, Jan. 1, 1808, the importation of slaves into the United States was prohibited by Congress.

There are a multitude more that might be added. Omar's words are wise: " Worship God; be not a worshipper of days."

Fountain Pens and Typewriters. — The fountain pen is not a recent invention.   In 1824 Thomas Jefferson saw one in use and wrote to General Bernard Peyton to get him one.   The first English patent for a fountain pen was granted in 1809; the first American one in 1830.   The first recorded patent for a typewriting machine is by an Englishman named Henry Mill, and is dated 1714.   In 1841 a Frenchman named Pierre Foucalt invented a practicable machine.   He was blind.   The modern machine is due to an American named Sholes, who brought it to perfection in 1873.

The Bicycle not a New Invention. — Evelyn's diary under the date of Aug. 4, 1665, speaks of examining at Durdans " a wheel for one to run races in," contrived by Dr. Wilkins, Sir William Petty, and Mr. Hooke, three men notable for " parts and ingenuity."   In a stained glass window at Stoke Poges, dating back to the seventeenth century, there is a representation of a mechanical wheel like a bicycle.   It is " really a cherub on Ezekiel's wheel."

The Dutch did not invent Thimbles. — A newspaper states " that the Dutch invented the thimble in 1690."   Thorold Rogers, in his " History of Agriculture and Prices in England," gives the quotation of a dozen thimbles, in 1494, as four shillings. Shakespeare speaks of them. Edward Peacock thinks that they were undoubtedly prehistoric.

Magnetic Mountains. — Readers of the "Arabian Nights" will remember the magnetic black mountain that drew all the nails out of the ships and caused them to fall to pieces. A Vienna newspaper says the island of Bornholm in the Baltic is a huge magnet that has sufficient power to deflect the needle and turn the vessel out of its course. The magnetic influence is felt at a distance of fifteen kilometers (nine miles and a half).

The Earth as a Conductor. — It is still supposed by many persons that the electrical conductivity of the earth is infinite. But it is a fact well ascertained that "in railway return circuits the earth return does more harm than good; for power service the earth is useless as a return, and in telegraphy alone it appears likely to serve a permanently useful purpose."

Electric Light in Fog. — The notion obtains in England that the electric light does not penetrate the fog. This is unfounded. Owing to this prejudice lighthouses furnished with electricity are fewer on the English coast than along the coast of France.

Depth of Coral Reefs. — Darwin's theory that coral reefs are formed by subsidence, the coral polyp building up as the land sank, has been recently disproved by borings. The great atoll on the Yucatan bank is only 32 fathoms deep. Those on the Solomon Islands are only from 125 to 130 feet deep; along the coast of Cuba only 145 feet; and along the coast of Florida only 60 feet. According to Darwin they should have been at least 2,000 feet. ·

The Weight of the Brain.—Advocates of the superiority of man over woman usually use, as an argument, the fact that man's brain weighs from one-ninth to one-twelfth more than the average woman's. Neither weight nor multiplicity of convolutions seems to be a safe criterion. The brain of the great chemist Liebig was below the average in weight. The brain of the elephant is richer in convolutions than man's.

Lead Shot.—It is generally supposed that lead shot are made spherical by falling, and that the shot towers are built for that purpose. They are more perfect in shape the instant they start than at any other time. But in falling the two hundred feet they cool and harden, and are received into water which acts as a cushion. Arsenic, mixed with the lead, causes the molten mass, when strained through a perforated receptacle, to form into globules.

The Horse-power of Guns.—It is a mistake to suppose that a large cannon is longer lived than a shot-gun. The "Engineering and Mining Journal" says that after about one hundred shots have been fired they are practically useless. Three hundred shots represent only one second of actual work! For a 100-ton gun with a 550-pound charge of

6824 ·

powder throws a projectile weighing 2,020 pounds at an initial velocity of 1,715 feet a second. The kinetic force employed in the one one-hundredth of a second is equivalent to 92,597,000 foot-pounds, or 17,000,000-horse power.

Bock Bier. — In spite of the brewers' pictures of a buck dancing on a barrel, the word bock in the spring-brewing of beer has no derivation to correspond with such art. It is said to be derived from the town of Eimbeck, in Hanover, where particularly strong beer was made. This was changed into *ein bock*, meaning a glass; but here the buck may be a pony.

Prussic Acid and Almonds. — A British newspaper, referring to the death of a bird, attributes it to the presence of prussic acid in a bitter almond. But in the natural state there is none. Prussic acid results from the manufacture of "oil of bitter almonds." The cake left after the natural oil has been pressed out contains two constituents called amygdaline and synaptase. When the cake is made into a paste with water, and allowed to remain at a moderately warm temperature, the synaptase causes the amygdaline to ferment and decompose into the volatile "oil of bitter almonds," and, among other substances, prussic or hyorocyanic acid. Neither the oil nor the poison is in the almonds originally; in fact, the latter contain not the slightest trace of either ready formed. The "Globe" Encyclopædia says: "Bitter almonds possess a poisonous principle

similar in effects to prussic acid," but while this
"poisonous principle" remains undefined, we are
not quite sure, supposing bitter almonds were eaten
in large quantities and remained long undigested,
that the formation of prussic acid in the way described would not actually be accelerated by the
warmth of the stomach.

Pulque Skins. — Pulque is sold at Mexican
railway stations in hog-skins or sheep-skins taken
whole from the animal. A popular explanation of
the mystery is that the creature is tied, with food
placed just beyond his reach. He struggles so hard
to get at it that he finally walks out of his skin,
leaving it whole behind him. This is an error!

CHAPTER VII.

WORDS, PHRASES, AND THINGS THAT ARE MIS-UNDERSTOOD.

"Born in the Purple." — The epithet porphyro-genitus — " born in the purple " — does not refer to the Roman or Grecian Imperial Court dye, but to the fact that the Empresses of Constantine's city, when they drew near the time of child-bearing, were lodged in the Porphyry Chamber. This was at the south-west corner of the palace, and its floors and walls were covered with purple marble. The title was first officially applied to Constantine VII., — Constantine Porphyrogenitus, — who reigned in the tenth century.

The Bar Sinister. — It is a mistake to speak of a bar sinister as a sign of bastardy. It is a false translation of the French *barre*, which means *bend sinister*.

Apologies do not imply Faults. — George the Third, when told that Bishop Watson had published " An Apology for the Bible," remarked that he did not know that the Bible needed an apology. The king did not realize that the word is also used in the old Greek sense of *defence*. Hence a Christian apologist is one who *defends*, not excuses; he does not admit the existence of fault in the Bible which he defends. The "Evidences of Christianity" are for the same reason technically called *apologetics*.

Epicures. — Epicure is very generally supposed to mean one whose chief pleasure is a voluptuous gratification of the appetite. The right definition is, one who, however humble his fare, will have it of the best of its kind. Rousseau said: "Abstaining, so as *really* to enjoy, is epicurism," and the "pleasure" which Epicurus, the apostle of temperance, with his barley cake and water, set before his apostles consisted of the pleasures of refinement perfected by reason, whether in eating or drinking, religion or politics, arts or science, or in the pleasures of wine and love.

Norsemen and Northmen. — The Norsemen were the Norwegians, who spoke a language called Norse; the Northmen were, of course, the ancient inhabitants of Northern Europe.

Do not say "Vi-king." — This word is not properly pronounced "vy-king," and does not mean a "sea-king." The appropriateness of this error has made it long-lived. The termination is "ing," not "king;" the syllable "vik" is the Norse word for "creek" or "cove," and "ing" for "sons" or "people." Wherefore "Vikings" means "sons or people of the creek."

A little more than Kin and less than Kind. — The word king is not, as is commonly supposed, derived from the Saxon *cunnan*, to know, as of one who has power or *can* because he kens or knows. It is allied with the Sanskrit *ganaka*, a father, from the word *gan*, to beget, akin with our kin. *Kin-ing* therefore means son of the *kin* or *tribe*, a chosen leader.

The Origin of Foolscap. — The following particulars were given in the " Lithographer," to account for the *origin* of this term: " Charles I. granted numerous monopolies for the support of the government, and among others was the manufacture of paper. The water-mark of the finest sort was the royal arms. This monopoly was set aside by the Parliament that brought Charles I. to the scaffold, and, by way of showing contempt for the king, they ordered the royal arms to be taken from the paper, and a fool, with his cap and bells, to be substituted. It is now over two hundred years since the fool's cap was taken from the paper, but still the size which the Rump Parliament ordered for their journals bears the name of the water-mark placed there as an indignity to Charles."

There is no truth in this frequently reiterated statement that the Rump Parliament placed a fool's cap on their own paper to spite the dead king. The cap and bells may account for the origin of the name foolscap, but the water-mark itself is still shrouded in mystery. The term was in use at least as early as 1659; and an alleged example of it, dated 1479, figures in a catalogue of an exhibition. There is no justification for the derivation from the Italian *foglio capo*.

The Flag that rules the Wave. — The "Jack," say most authorities, refers to James VI. of Scotland (James I. of England), whose signature was always "Jacques." It was so called because used as a "jack" — that is, in sea language, a flag displayed from the end of a staff on a bowsprit; hence the name "Union Jack" has come to be applied on land to the larger "union" flag itself. The opinion is to some extent confirmed by the sailors' personification of the yellow fever into "Yellow Jack," which at first was merely a yellow flag or jack.

"Tun" and its Meaning. — Many grammars say tun, at the end of names, signifies "town" or "village." But "tun" was really the name of a single Saxon homestead. The popular accounts of the depopulation of the New Forest by William I. are thus brought at least within the bounds of credibility.

Cinderella's Glass Slipper. — Unimaginative etymologists have done their best to destroy the poetic beauty of Cinderella's slipper by arguing that the words *la petite pantoufle de verre* — the little glass slipper — as found in Perrault's story, published in 1697, should be *pantoufle de vair, vair* being a kind of fur — miniver or weasel. But surely if the slipper had been of fur the sisters would have had no trouble in forcing their toes into it. Moreover, the fairy godmother who could change a pumpkin into a coach, and mice into horses, would not hesitate to give Cinderella slippers of glass, spun glass, perhaps, and flexible.

Wainscot. — In Walter M. Skeat's Etymological Dictionary " wainscot " is derived from Dutch *wagen*, a wain or wagon. He himself became convinced that this popular derivation is wrong, and his later edition attributes it to the Middle Dutch *waeg*, a wall.

Creoles. — Strictly speaking, a creole is the offspring of European parents, though now the term is used in the colonies as a general designation for anything West Indian, negro, and English, animal and vegetable alike ; thus, " creole mutton," " creole cat," and " creole basket." Hence it has come to mean a person of white and black parentage, born in the West Indies or South America. This is wrong, for such a one is a mulatto. The Standard Dictionary gives the derivation of the word from criollo, a negro ; and that from creado, a servant, from crear, to create. But this is doubtful.

Cyclones, Tornadoes, and Hurricanes. — These three words are usually confused except in scientific writings. A cyclone is a storm covering a vast extent of country — some are one or two thousand miles in diameter — and having a system of winds that blow spirally, although, owing to the great extent of the storm, the wind at any particular place seems to be blowing straight ahead. A tornado, on the other hand, is a fierce whirlwind, the path of which is generally only a few rods wide,

It sometimes travels many miles, destroying everything in its course. A funnel-shaped cloud formed
by condensed vapor, and clouds of dust in the very
core of the tornado, are its distinguishing feature.
In the infantile days of language-study hurricane
was supposed to be a storm that harried plantations and hurried the cane ! In other words, raised
Cain with them. The word is really a West Indian
word. In Irving's " Columbus " it says that the
awful whirlwinds that " occasionally rage within
the tropics " were called by the Indians " furicanes "
or " uricans." The word is said to be the name of
the tempest god Hurikon.

Piazza.—This Italian word denotes what the
Spanish call *plaza*, French *place*, and the English a *square*. Architecturally it means an arcade,
a portico, or covered walk supported by columns.
In the United States it has come to mean a verandah
or porch, or even a balcony.

A Chateau is not necessarily a Castle. —
What the French call château, unless it be in
Spain, generally signifies a large stone farmhouse.

Mephistopheles a Devil, but not the Devil. —
This fiendish character in Goethe's " Faust " was
not the devil, but only *one* of the devil's many
mediæval assistants.

CHAPTER VIII.

MISTAKES WE MAKE IN CONNECTION WITH ANCIENT HISTORY.

Thothmes the Third not to be compared with Alexander. — Miss Amelia B. Edwards, in her "Pharaohs, Fellahs and Explorers" (p. 160), says: "Thothmes the Third was the Alexander of ancient Egyptian history. He conquered the known world of his day; he carved the names of six hundred and twenty-eight vanquished nations and captured cities on the walls of Karnak; and he set up a tablet of victory in the Great Temple."

But Prof. George Rawlinson says his task was trivial as compared with that of the Macedonian general, and his achievements were insignificant. Instead of plunging with a small force into the midst of populous countries, and contending with armies ten or twenty times as large as his own, defeating them, and utterly subduing a vast empire, Thothmes marched at the head of a numerous disciplined army into thinly peopled regions, governed by petty chiefs jealous of one another, fought scarcely a single great battle, and succeeded in conquering two regions of a moderate size, Syria and Mesopotamia.

Alexander overran and subdued the entire tract between the Ægean and the Sutlej, the Persian Gulf and the Oxus. Thothmes subdued not a tenth part of the space, and the empire which he established did not endure for more than a century.

Alexander conquered Egypt and founded a dynasty there which lasted for nearly three centuries. It is thus absurd to compare the third Thothmes with the great Alexander in the light of a conqueror.

Forgetting that he was a first-rate administrator, we are inclined to think of Alexander as only a victor. He so organized the East that it continued for nearly three centuries, and mainly under Greek rule. Thothmes, on the contrary, organized nothing. He left his conquests in such a condition that at his death all of them revolted and had to be reestablished.

Alexander did not weep for Other Worlds to conquer. — Plutarch says: "Alexander wept when he heard[1] that there was an infinite number of worlds, and his friends asking him if any accident had befallen him, he returns this answer: 'Do you not think it a matter worthy of lamentation that when there is such a vast number of them, we have not yet conquered one?'"

Alexander did not "weep for other worlds to conquer," but because his ambition was so far from being realized in this.

---

[1] From Anaxarchus, his favorite philosopher, who accompanied the Asiatic expeditions.

There is good reason to suspect that in India his army met with serious reverses, which induced him to retrace his steps.

The Story of Troy a Myth. — Able historians have tried to fix the time of the siege of Troy, and have argued in favor of at least a dozen dates between 1335 and 1149 B.C. According to Homer's account, Helen must have been not less than sixty years old when Paris fell in love with her, but then she was supposed to partake with Castor and Pollux of immortality. Recent discoverers have found remains of a number of large cities on the supposed site of Ilion.

The Battle of Thermopylæ. — History states that in 480 B.C. a small army of Greeks under Leonidas defended the pass of Thermopylæ against a vast army under Xerxes (Khshayârshâ) — the Biblical Ahasuerus. Their position was betrayed, and Leonidas sent away his troops, except 300 Spartans and 700 Thespians, who remained to defend the pass, and were slain. But modern investigators have proved that Xerxes' army was grossly exaggerated, and that it was not stopped by 1,000 men, but by 7,000, or even, as some authors compute, by 12,000. Moreover, the Spartan contingent showed no more bravery in this conflict than their companions in arms.

Archimedes and his Circles. — It is undoubtedly a historical fact that Archimedes met his death when the Romans under Marcellus attacked and captured Syracuse, 212 B.C. But the story that he was engaged in mathematical work, and was busy contemplating certain circles drawn in the sand when a Roman soldier appeared, may or may not be true. "Do not disturb my circles!" the philosopher is said to have exclaimed, but the soldier struck him down. This is a pretty fiction. So also is the story of his great burning glass which burned the ships of the Romans in the harbor. The circumstances are impossible. The story that he said, "Give me a *pou sto* and I will move the world," is another invention of later days.

The Gate of Janus. — The strange Roman god Janus, with two faces, had a gateway close by the Forum dedicated to his honor by King Numa; but there is no reason for styling it Janus' Temple, unless because it contained a bronze statue of the god, and thus became a sacred place. It was merely an archway with two doors, one on a side, closed in time of peace, and opened only in time of war. An Etruscan god, with two or four faces, was identified with Janus, hence the plastic representation. The word Janus is another form of Dianus, the sun, just as the associated goddess Jana is Diana, the moon. But the later Romans connected the name with Janua, a door, hence the name of the month January. As the god of all beginnings, he was regarded with special reverence. A temple to him was built by Caius Duilius at the time of the first Punic war; this was restored by Augustus and dedicated by Tiberius.

Rose not a Flower. — The English given name Rose is by some believed to be derived from the Teutonic *hròs*, meaning fame, just as Rosamond is *hròs-mund*, " famed protection," and not " chaste rose." Nor is there any rose in the Rosetta stone; its name is a corruption of the Arabic *rashid*, glorious.

A Left-handed Yarn. — Many stories have been invented to explain the apparent meanings of proper names. Thus the Roman family name Scævola, which means the Left Handed, is accounted for by the familiar legend retold by Macaulay in his " Lays of Ancient Rome." It is said that in 509 B.C. Mucius Scævola made his way into the camp of King Porsena to kill him, while he was besieging Rome. But he killed instead a royal secretary, whom he mistook for the king. He was threatened with death by fire unless he revealed the details of a conspiracy, whereupon he thrust his right hand into the fire prepared for him and burnt it off. This firmness allayed the suspicions and excited the admiration of Porsena, who ordered his release. The story of Tarquin's insult to Lucretia is also a legend. Tarquin's power may have been overthrown by a popular insurrection, but its cause was not that given in the poem of Shakespeare.

Horatius and the Bridge. — Macaulay in another lay tells

> " How well Horatius kept the bridge
> In the brave days of old."

Horatius never defended the bridge over the Tiber against the Etruscans; neither did the mother of Coriolanus intercede with her son to spare Rome. The story is a modern fabrication.

Sappho did not commit Suicide. — About 600 B.C. flourished the famous Grecian lyric poetess Sappho, or Psappha, as she called herself in her own Æolic dialect. The ancients delighted to call her "The Poet," so unique was her renown. There is no foundation for the story that she was a wanton beauty who threw herself from the Leucadian promontory into the sea, out of love for a beautiful youth, Phason, who disdained her advances. Late investigations prove her to have been a respectable married woman with a large family, which she raised with as much care as a Greek matron usually bestowed on her children.

It is not too commonly known that her nine books of lyric poems were burnt by some anti-Pagan fanatic. Scaliger says that Pope Gregory VII. was the miscreant, in the year 1073; but Mr. N. T. Wharton rejects this as lacking confirmatory evidence, and offers the alternative story of Cardan, who gives 380 as the year of the burning, under Gregory Nazianzen.

All that are left to us are her "Ode to Aphrodite," and the fragmentary allusions and quotations from her works by ancient writers.

Romulus a Myth. — The beautiful story of Romulus and Remus suckled by the she-wolf, and their quarrel, and the foundation of the city of Rome, has no historic foundation. The first person to relate it lived hundreds of years after the reputed A.U.C.

Dido and the Hide. — The story of Dido winning land at Carthage by cutting oxhides into strips and thus enclosing a considerable space arises from the misinterpretation of the word *byrsa*, a Greek mispronunciation of the Semitic *birctha*, a citadel. The story reappears in connection with many cities and castles, even as late as the eleventh century, when Hasan ben Sabah in this way is said to have secured the castle of Alamùt in Northern Persia, where he established himself as the Sheikh ul Jebal, the Head of the Assassins.

Origin of the Irish. — The legend that the Irish are of Phœnician origin is said to have arisen from the similarity of sound in the Irish word *fena*, plural *fion*, beautiful, agreeable.

Diogenes' Tub a Myth. — The same year that Alexander died at Babylon Diogenes died at Corinth, 323 B.C.; but not in a tub, because he never lived in one. The story originated in a comment by his biographer, Seneca, who was not born till more than three hundred years after the cynic's death: "A man so crabbed ought to have lived in a tub like a dog."

Æsop's Fables. — The story of Æsop the lame slave who is commonly reputed to be the author of the fables is much involved in legend. He was very probably not a historical personage. Many if

not all of his fables are of more ancient date.   Miss
Amelia B. Edwards says: "Some of the fables attributed to him are drawn from Egyptian sources
older by eight hundred years than the famous
dwarf who is supposed to have invented them.   The
fable of the 'Lion and the Mouse' was discovered
by Dr. Brugsch in an Egyptian papyrus a few years
ago.   'The Dispute of the Stomach and the Members' has been yet more recently identified by Professor Maspero with an ancient Egyptian original."

Seneca a Usurer. — Seneca was not the half-
Christian philosopher of whose virtues we are often
told, but a grasping usurer who died worth over
$3,000,000.   Nor was Cæsar Augustus a public
benefactor: he was the most exacting tax collector
of history.

The Hannibal Fable. — In 216 B.C. Hannibal
with about 50,000 men nearly annihilated the
Roman army of about 90,000 at Cannæ, in Apulia,
Italy; but it is all a fable to say that he sent
back to Carthage as evidence of his victory three
bushels of gold rings plucked from the hands of
dead Roman knights.   The messenger that carried
the news to the Carthaginian Senate, on concluding
his report, "opened his robe and threw out a number of gold rings gathered on the field of battle."

The Colossus of Rhodes. — There is no prob-
ability that such a statue as is usually represented
in pictures as straddling the entrance to the port
of Rhodes ever existed.

Words falsely attributed to Cæsar. — There is no historical foundation for the story that when Cæsar in 49 B.C. reached the Rubicon he communed with himself, saying in effect: " There is still time to turn back; one step further and civil war breaks forth; " then, taking a sudden resolution, he marched forward, exclaiming, " *Alea jacta est!* " " The die is cast!" "He plunged, he crossed, and Rome was free no more." Moreover, the Rubicon lay on the opposite side of the Italian peninsula from where he entered Italy. Neither did Cæsar exclaim, " *Et tu, Brute!* " when he was assassinated March 15, 44 B.C. Suetonia says Cæsar drew a deep sigh, but said not a word.

Lies about Cleopatra. — Cleopatra killed herself, 30 B.C., to avoid being exhibited at Rome in the triumph of Octavius, who had made war upon her and Antony because the latter had divorced his (Octavius') sister on the queen's account. But did she die from the bite of an asp? Rawlinson argues against it in his " Herod II.": " If her death had been caused by any serpent, the small viper would rather have been chosen than the large asp; but the story is disproved by her having decked herself in ' the royal ornaments,' and being found dead ' without any marks of suspicion of poison on her body.' "

Death from a serpent's bite could not have been mistaken, and her vanity would not have allowed her to choose one which would have disfigured her so frightfully.

No boy would have ventured to carry an asp in a basket of figs, some of which he offered to the guards as he passed. Even Plutarch shows that the story of the asp was doubted. Nor is the fact that the statue carried in Augustus' triumph had an asp upon it any proof of his belief in it, since the snake was the emblem of Egyptian royalty. The statue (or the crown) of Cleopatra could not have been without one, and this was probably the origin of the whole story.

Who has not heard of Cleopatra's pearl which, at a banquet given in Antony's honor, she dissolved in vinegar? Either this story also is fictitious, or vinegar was different in those days from the present-day kind, which will not melt pearls; nor will it split rocks, as it is made to do in the story of "Hannibal crossing the Alps."

Nero not such a Bad Fellow. — Another royal suicide was the Emperor Nero, who stabbed himself 68 A.D. He was not quite so bad a monster as the author of "Quo Vadis" would have us imagine. His mother, Agrippina, was not put to death by his order, nor did he play on his harp, and sing "The Burning of Troy" while Rome was on fire.

Our knowledge of him is gained mostly from Tacitus, who hated him, and from Petronius Arbiter, who was put to death for conspiracy against him. Hodgkin, in "Italy and her Invaders," says: "Even in Rome itself the common people strewed flowers on the grave of Nero."

CHAPTER IX.

THE MISTAKES WE MAKE IN RELIGIOUS HISTORY.

Israelites did not exterminate the Canaanites. — It is a common belief, but erroneous, that the Israelites exterminated the Canaanites. The Israelites, by force of arms, were a dominant caste, and *ruled over* the more civilized Canaanites.

Moses had no Horn. — The Hebrew for "shone" is *qâran*, to emit rays; for a horn, is *qeren*. The early translators confused the two by translating the passage in Exodus describing Moses on his descent from Sinai as *facies cornuta*, "his face was horned," instead of "his face shone." Hence artists have represented Moses with a horn, as if it referred to his power symbolized.

Christ was born 4 B.C. — Through the erroneous time fixed by the calculations of Dionysius, the date generally assigned for the nativity of our Lord is at least four years later than it should be. It must have preceded the death of Herod, who died four years before the beginning of the Christian era. After giving data upon which the later computation is founded, Farrar, in his "Life of Christ," adds: "Under no circumstances can it have taken place later than February, B.C. 4." So that instead of this being the year 1898, we should sign our letters 1902.

The Wise Men of the East. — In early Christian art few subjects have been oftener painted than the worship of the infant Saviour at Bethlehem by the wise men or " kings." [1]

In these early representations, and those of the Roman catacombs, the number of Magi varies, and when the words of St. Matthew are literally followed there are no signs of royalty. In one painting there are four, in another — in the chapel of S. Pietro e S. Marcellino — only two are shown. There is no biblical authority for fixing any number at all to the Magi of the gospel narrative. St. Matthew, the only evangelist who mentions them, says: " There came wise men from the east to Jerusalem." The idea that they were three in number no doubt is founded upon the three kinds of gifts they offered — gold, frankincense, and myrrh; at least this was the teaching of St. Augustine. It may also have some mystical connection with the idea of the Trinity.

The First Easter. — It is sometimes said that the first Easter was in the spring of the year 29 of our era. The crucifixion took place on the 7th of April of the Julian year, or the 5th of April according to the Gregorian reckoning, in 30 A.D.

---

[1] Psalm LXXII., 10, 11. " The kings of Tarshish and of the isles shall bring presents: the kings of Sheba and Seba shall offer gifts." Recited by Roman Catholics on the Feast of Epiphany.

Belial was the Father of no Sons. — The expression sons of Belial, or children of Belial, with the marginal rendering "naughty men," gives readers of the Bible the impression that Belial was a person or a god. It is really a Hebrew word meaning useless, hence "good for nothing."

Mary Magdalene. — Many persons, without any justification, identify the woman taken in adultery, as related in the eighth chapter of St. John, with Mary Magdalene, of whom nothing is known more than that seven devils were cast out of her (Luke VIII., 2); that she was present at Jesus' execution (Matthew XXVII., 56); and that Christ appeared first to her (Matthew XXVIII., 1). The term Magdalen, therefore, as applied to a fallen woman is an unjust stigma.

The Athanasian Creed. — The "Athanasian" Creed is not the production of the Alexandrian bishop whose name it bears, though it correctly expresses his doctrines. The original was written in Latin, not, as it would have been, in Greek, had Athanasius written it; in fact, it was entirely unknown in the language of the Greek Church up to the tenth century, and even in Latin did not appear before the end of the eighth century, whereas Athanasius lived in the fourth.

The Origin of the Papacy. — Roman Catholic controversialists urge that the Papacy was created by the Founder of Christianity; Protestant prejudices attribute it to designing priests. Its growth was rather the inevitable product of mediæval conditions. Ferdinand Gregorovius, in his "History of the City of Rome in the Middle Ages," points out the fact that the Bishop of Rome was the one rallying-point in a world of confusion, the one centre of order amid chaos, the one central light in a night of darkness. After describing the final sacking of the city of Rome he says: "Classical civilization perished in Rome and throughout Italy. In cities burnt, desolated, and mutilated, ruins remained the sole evidences of former splendor. The night of barbarism had descended on the Latin world, a darkness in which no light was visible other than that of the tapers of the church and the lonely student lamp of the monk brooding in his cloister."

Barbarians swarmed over Italy; the seat of empire was transferred to Byzantium; the Exarchate of Ravenna, which represented imperial rule in Italy, was powerless to stem the torrent of anarchy, and the ancient Roman Curia had perished. No authority remained save that which rested in the person of the Bishop of Rome, whose see thus gradually became the one object of obedience and highest veneration throughout Western Christendom, and who, therefore, naturally became the head of the Holy Roman Church. That power was more firmly secured by temporal possessions, partly gifts to the Roman see, and partly territories acquired by diplomacy of the bishops when popes. By the end of the eighth century the Temporal Power was established largely by the reciprocal aid of one of the world's most noted rulers — the emperor of the German Western Empire, Charles the Great.

Is the Pope Infallible ? — In calling the pope infallible Roman Catholics mean that God preserves him from *erring* in expounding Holy Scripture, and in teaching points of faith or of morals, when he does all this *ex cathedrâ.* The Pope is not regarded as impeccable ; that is, preserved from *sinning.* In a somewhat like manner in civil matters a judge may be blamable in his private life, and yet eminent and faultless in his official duty of deciding points of civil law.

" Saint " and " Holy." — The famous mosque at Constantinople was not called so for any " saint " of the name of " Sophia." The church was originally dedicated by Constantine the Great to " sacred or holy wisdom," *Hagia Sophia ;* that is, to Christ, as the personified wisdom of God. Among other instances where " Saint " does not mean " saint," but " holy," we have St. Sepulchre, Protestant churches at London and Cambridge, St. Croix River in Wisconsin, and Sainte Chapelle at Paris, built by St. Louis to receive and enshrine the crown of thorns. St. Mary, when used for Roman Catholic churches, means " Holy " Mary, as the reverence there paid her is much greater than the word " saint " would imply.

Auto de fe. — The first *auto de fe* was at Valladolid in May, 1559, and was witnessed by Philip

II., the Prince of the Asturias.   Another took place in Seville, Dec. 22, 1560; thirteen were burnt to death, four in effigy.   It is a mistake to use the particle *da* or to put an acute accent over *fe*.   The words are Spanish, and signify act of faith.

No Woman was ever Pope. — A story was at one time popularly believed, that a beautiful and learned German woman named Joanna, born at Mayence or Ingelheim, fell in love with a recreant monk, and escaping with him in man's attire travelled through France, Italy, and Greece.   After the lover died in Athens, Joanna came to Rome, and, still keeping up the fiction of her assumed sex under the name of Angelicas, established a school there.   After the death of Pope Leo IV. in 855, she was unanimously elected pope and took the appellation of Johann VIII.   Her rule was, after two years and six months, interrupted by a scandal; an angel appeared to her and offered her the choice of being damned in the next world or acknowledging her transgression in this.   She accordingly joined in a procession, was taken with the pangs of child-birth on the way between the Coliseum and the Chapel of St. Clement, and died, and was buried without any honors, after a pontificate of nearly two years and a half; and on the spot a chapel was erected which succeeding popes always avoided.   The first historian to mention this fable was Marianus Scotus, but others made capital of it. Of course as Leo IV. died July 17, 855, and Benedict III. succeeded him, reigning till 858, there could have been no place for Joanna. The ceremony of the *sedia stercoraria* from which the story may have arisen was discontinued in the sixteenth century. Some attribute the rise of the story to the effeminacy or licentiousness of Pope John XII., who was killed in 964 while prosecuting a conspiracy against the Emperor of Germany, Otto I.

Nuns were never "walled up." — Despite the fate of Constance de Beverly, as depicted in Scott's "Marmion," monks and nuns have never been walled up alive, as many still believe, by the Roman Catholic Church. The word *murus*, a wall, used as a substantive in mediæval Latin and all the derivative tongues, signified prison, and *murato*, put in walls, did not necessarily mean walled up, any more than immured means walled up in England.

Mr. Rider Haggard, in his novel "Montezuma's Daughter," has confessed that, even if the taking of the life of a nun for a grave moral transgression might be conceivably defended as an act of judicial authority, there is no proof that such a barbarous punishment was ever enforced. There was a time when foundations were actually laid with the sacrificial blood and other remains of human bodies. From this circumstance originated the superstition that to secure the permanence of bridges, castles, and other great structures, it was necessary to build up the body of a live child or maiden in the foundations.

This belief has survived for many centuries in Europe, and was invoked to account for every skeleton found in an unusual part of any religious or other old building.

Helena not a Briton. — The story that Helena, the mother of Constantine the Great, and the collector of so many Christian relics, was a British lady rests on no good authority. There is good reason to believe that she was really the daughter of an innkeeper at Antioch.

Dives not a Proper Name. — The name "Dives" is generally supposed to have been the surname of the rich man at whose door Lazarus lay, and is therefore improperly printed with a capital "D." There is no such name in Scripture. The painted representation of this parable was a favorite with the monks, and under it they inscribed in Latin,. *Dives* (the rich man) *et Lazarus*, hence the misapprehension. The correct pronunciation of this name is di-vēs, not dives.

Parsis not Fire-worshippers. — The Parsî is unjustly called a fire-worshipper. Yet to him fire is but the emblem of the power of God, whom he worships as devoutly as Christians do the God of the Bible. The name Parsî is only another form of Farsî or Persian, and is borne by the descendants of those who at the Muhammadan Conquest took the religion of Zoroaster (Zarathustra) down into India.

Juggernaut not a Fetish. — It has been told that the worshippers of Juggernaut throw themselves under the wheels of the car by the score, in the belief that they will thus obtain eternal salvation. The car is taken out only about once in thirty years, and the deaths which the old missionary stories and pictures so exaggerated were generally accidental. The two or three exceptional victims of self-immolation chose this manner of death to free themselves from excruciating complaints. Even in the last reincarnation year of Juggernaut (1893), with every precaution, accidents were barely avoided, but in old days with no police this was impossible.

Savonarola not the Precursor of Protestantism. — Savonarola was a contemporary of Columbus. Popular histories, text-books, and the like, often call him " among the leaders of the Reformation," or say that " he was a harbinger of the Reformation," or that he is " rightly called a precursor of Protestantism." It would be very easy to pile up instance upon instance of this ignorance, this misunderstanding of the great reformer's work.

Savonarola's life and words preclude the idea that he was a " harbinger" of the Protestant Reformation. But he was a " great reformer" of the evil lives of men in high places. Like Nehemiah, he preached against abuses. Yet Savonarola's own works show that he would have regarded the sixteenth century Reformation as an act of apostasy. As to his contempt for the reformers with whom he is so frequently ticketed, how do we find him in every page of his history? Saying mass, believing in transubstantiation, devoted to the Virgin, dutifully submitting to the rules of his order, and participating in all the ceremonies of the Roman Church as they are performed to-day, and, unlike Martin Luther of the next half century, keeping his religious vows till his death. He was disobedient to the Pope, but his disobedience was through misapprehension, and therefore can hardly be called heretical.

Muhammad was not a Miracle-worker. — The Christian's notion of Muhammad the Prophet of Islâm is that he was an impostor and fanatic. The most curious thing about him is that he himself never claimed any supernatural powers, and that the attribute of miracles to the prophet is not warranted by the Koran.

Moreover, the earliest life of Muhammad makes very little mention of miracles, and all those which are associated with his name are the creation of later biographers, who accurately gauged the taste for sensational details.

The Kingdom of Prester John. — The legend of a Christian sovereign called Prester or Presbyter Johannes, ruling in Central Asia, grew out of a name. It may have been Bahram Gur; or a chief named Gur Khan (meaning universal Khan), which was twisted into Yurkhan and Juchanan, hence Johannes. Other writers have tried to find the origin of the myth in John Orbelian of Georgia. Probably some rumor of Jenghis Khan was foundation for the story, which is attributed to the Bishop of Gabala.

St. Augustine did not introduce Christianity into England. — Many persons confuse St. Augustine, the first Archbishop of Canterbury, about 600, with St. Augustine, the celebrated Father of the Latin Church, who died 430, and believe that the author of the celebrated confessions introduced Christianity into England. There had been fifteen archbishops of London before then; and — to say nothing about the primitive churches of Ireland and Scotland — there were three sees, with cathedrals, in the province of Caerleon, or Wales, before Augustine saw the white cliffs of Albion. Bæda said that Ethelbert gave Augustine and his people, on his conversion, power to restore the churches. The word restore implies their previous existence. Was there an accidental Christian colony in Canterbury, or was there a British Christian Church before the Saxons came?

Bruno was not burnt Alive. — In 1587 the philosopher, Giordano Bruno, was lecturing at the University of Wittenberg. About his death there is a very common error. Flammarion in his "Popular Astronomy," 1894, still further spreads it. It is to the effect that Bruno "was burned alive at Rome before the terrified people," because he asserted the stars to be the centres of other systems.

The charge laid against Bruno was not the one mentioned; and it is extremely doubtful whether he met with scientific martyrdom at all, the sole evidence of his execution being a letter of Scioppius, the genuineness of which has been seriously called to question by Professor Desdouits.

It is certain that he left Italy to avoid the consequences of publicly denouncing the doctrines of transubstantiation and of the immaculate conception, and that on his return to Naples, some years later, he was arrested by order of the Inquisition, as an unbeliever, and especially as being the author of "The Expulsion of the Triumphant Beast," "Spaccio della bestia Trionfante," written in London while under the protection of the French Ambassador, 1584.

The "Italian missionary" (as Dean Hook calls St. Augustine) found himself in conflict with the British bishops almost as soon as he landed. And his failure to bring the British church into union with that of Canterbury was lamentable.

Mr. Newel, after examining various hypotheses, is inclined to trace British Christianity to a Gallican origin. Christianity was founded in these islands toward the close of the second and the beginning of the third centuries, and was probably brought from the Rhône Valley after the persecution of the year 177. Some of the persecuted Gallican Christians fled through Arles and Lyons to Britain. "In default of genuine tradition," writes Mr. Newel, "respecting the origin of the British church, it appears most probable that the Christian missionaries came that way from the churches of the Rhône Valley to Britain."

Canterbury is not the First Christian Church in England. — Canterbury is not "the first Christian Church in England." The honor belongs rather to Glastonbury, the *vetusta ecclesia* — the wicker church — founded by St. Patrick, the apostle of Ireland, more than a century before Pope Gregory sent missionaries to those whom he declared to be " *non Angli sed Angeli.*"

CHAPTER X.

MISTAKES IN ENGLISH HISTORY.

We are not descended from the Celts. — The ancient Britons are usually called Celts or Kelts, but the ancient Kelts probably never came into Briton at all. Their peculiar skulls are not found there either in river-bed or barrow. Northern Europe was represented by the ancients as occupied by the Celts — the Western people — and the Scythians — the Eastern people. The Rhine came to be considered the eastern frontier of the Celts, and Celtica, in the time of Cæsar, was called Gaul. The British Islands were never included in the term, and were distinctly stated to be outside of and "opposite" Celtica. Cæsar refers to the Celtæ as a definite race occupying central France.

Wherefore the term "Kelt" should be applied to the Britons, not as a distinct race, but as a people speaking one of the European languages which philologists have merely for convenience chosen to call Keltic.[1] The Britons of pre-Roman and pre-Saxon times were not Kelts *because* they spoke Keltic, any more than an Indian is "Anglo-Saxon"

---

[1] Similarly the term "Aryan" can only be used in a linguistic sense.

because he speaks English. If language were a test of race, it would be quite allowable to class the Irish of Dublin and the Shetland folk as English.

The Picts were not Painted. — Lord Strangford says: " The Picts got their name from the Romans, as being tattooed distinct from the clothed and tamed Britons."   An English Board School " Historical Reader " says, " but the Picts — the Painted Men — came pouring in over the old Roman walls." This derivation is noticed by Claudian, who speaks of the Picts as *nec falso nomine Picti*. All the early Roman and Irish chronicles perpetuate his derivation of the word.

It is taken for granted that because the Picts painted or stained themselves, their name means "the painted." The Romans could scarcely have used it in specializing one tribe in the north of Britain, while at a much earlier date they were familiar with the custom of tattooing practised by other tribes in the south ; therefore the southern Britons ought to have been the true Picts.

There is little doubt that the name was the original tribal name *peicta* slightly altered in the mouths of the Romans, and meant " fighters," the term being traceable to the Gaelic *peicta* or the Welsh *peith*, a " fighting man," — a root related to the Latin *pugna*. That they were preëminent fighters, of huge stature, is no speculation, but a historical fact based on the scanty records of Roman writers. And of the invincible Attacott Picts it is told that,

so valued was their prowess, they were drilled
with the Roman cohorts, and fought under the mas-
terly lead of Kenneth MacEdairn for the Emperor
Honorius.

The Britons were not driven into Wales. —
An English historical reader, following the usual
statement, declares that when the Anglo-Saxons
conquered Britain "the native Britons, or Welsh,
as the English called them, were driven into
Wales." All the rest were killed. This theory
of extermination and expatriation is proved by
Professor Huxley, Dr. Rolleston, Dr. Beddoe, and
other competent investigators to be utterly false.

The examination of burial places in the so-called
"Anglo-Saxon" period shows that the Britons and
their conquerors continued to live on side by side;
and the modern Englishman shows every grada-
tion of type which would be produced by the inter-
marriage of such people as the dark-haired, long-
headed Briton, and those of Roman admixture,
with the light-haired, broad-headed Saxon. Moreover we are expressly told in the English "Chronicle" that the lineage of the Saxon kings and the
royal families of the Strathclyde Britons was often
blended.

Our "Anglo-Saxon" ancestors called the "Kelts"
Wealas, Welshmen (the singular of which is
wealh), which means foreigners, just as the
Germans call Italy Wälschland. Bæda mentions
how the Saxon king, Eadwine of York, rendered

most of the Welsh abbots tributaries to his race. William of Malmesbury, four centuries later, can hardly transcribe in his classical Latin the names of Welsh abbots, " because they smack of British barbarism." Again he says: " The English and Britons *joined together* against him (Ceawlin), and his army was put to flight at Wodnesdic," which was about one hundred years after the popular date of the first Saxon settlement. Besides, as the Angles or Saxons took at least four hundred years to do what they did, and appeared only after long intervals, without any semblance to concerted action, it must have been physically impossible to drive the Britons *en masse* into the Welsh mountains; to admit the possibility of such a feat is to credit the invaders with the ability to do without what both the earlier Romans and the later Normans found to be a very exacting necessity, namely, dependence upon the conquered.

Had the Britons all been displaced, the names of the towns would have disappeared also; but the most ancient cities of the Roman occupation retained, and still retain, their Welsh names — Colchester, Winchester, Worcester, and an immense number of others, in which the first syllable, the real name, is unaltered, and the second is merely an Anglicized form of the Roman *castra*. Even Mr. Freeman admits that some of the cities may have been tributary to the English rather than occupied by them.

Again, almost every English river where the settlers were thickest bears a British name; and our oldest existing documents prove that when the English renamed a place, that name was contemporaneous with a Welsh one. It is asked: "If the British survived in comparatively large numbers, why is our language wholly a Teutonic tongue?"

The most plausible answer is: "Consider what language the Mashonas will speak in a few generations; consider whether the thousands of tourists who visit Wales ever trouble to learn even Welsh place names; think of the Englishman's island — Anglesey; its very name spells annihilation, and yet it need hardly be said that the population still remains essentially Welsh."

It would seem, therefore, preferable to believe that when the English colonized Britain they enslaved rather than exterminated the mass of the population.

The Saxons did not land when the Romans left. — Historians have asserted that the Saxons landed in Britain *after* the Romans had left it unprotected. This statement conveys a false impression. There is little doubt that the Saxon tribes had settled on the maritime parts of Britain long *before* the landing of Cæsar. Else it cannot be understood how the Romans should have met with such stubborn resistance, and not infrequent reverses, if the defenders had as weapons only the clubs of the primitive savages, instead of the superior Saxon weapons.

In burial grounds dating from pre-Roman times two distinct types of skull are found; the short-headed ones are accompanied by superior weapons. This coincides with Cæsar's account. He says: "The natives of the interior were indigenous, and the coast people — totally different — had crossed over from the neighborhood of Belgium."

Tacitus, writing one hundred and fifty years later, gives testimony to the same effect. The title "Comes Litoris Saxonici," given to the Roman governors of the coast tribes, — two of whom are known by their Germanic names, — shows that the Romans actually found it expedient to prevent further Saxon immigrations.

Pearson ("History of England," I., 6) says: "The Saxons of the fifth century seem to have found a kindred people already established in East Anglia, since no conquest of that district is on record."

The English are not an Anglo-Saxon People. — Tennyson, in his "Welcome to Alexandra," says:

> "Saxon and Norman and Dane are we,
> But all of us Danes in our welcome of thee."

And with a still further enlargement of the idea at the end of the poem:

> "For Saxon or Dane or Norman we,
> Teuton or Celt, or whatever we be,
> We are each all Dane in our welcome of thee,
>   Alexandra."

The term " Anglo-Saxon " is frequently applied
to the English, but the English are not an " Anglo-
Saxon," but an Anglo-British, people. The Roman
half-breed and the pure Briton after the evacuation
made too stout a resistance to be effaced by the
Saxons. The Roman element may be recognized by
its influence in the English municipal institutions;
in not a few towns, such as London, York, Leicester, and Exeter, we see distinctly that the Roman
legacy was never practically broken.

The dominant legal and religious traditions
remain unbroken, and so the dominant racial element in the British Isles to-day is not Saxon, but
British, or, in deference to popular parlance, Keltic. Considering that the Angles and Saxons were
one and the same people, it would be well to
eliminate one of the names — " Saxon," for preference. Their own name was probably " Angles; "
" Saxon" was only another name given to them
by the Britons as a common expression for
any invader. The Romans in Britain always
called " Saxons" those people whom we are accustomed to name " Angles." As the Angles and
Britons became blended, the two words became
interchangeable, and Latin writers of a later period,
to avoid confusion, naturally wrote *Angli-Saxones*.

**King Alfred did not burn the Cakes or enact
Good Laws.** — The story that King Alfred
allowed the cakes to burn, or that he ventured
into the Danish camp disguised as a minstrel, has

no historical foundation, though it frequently appears in books written for children. A students' history states that he enacted good laws. The Oxford Local Examiners, in their annual report for 1894, found occasion to deplore similar misinformation. The fact is that as a legislator Alfred added nothing to existing laws, but simply revised those of his predecessors, keeping "those that seemed to him good," rejecting "those that seemed to him not good," and combining the former into a single code.

Ethelred not Unready. — Ethelred's epithet, "Unready," had not the modern meaning, *unprepared*, that so many school-books state, but referred to the king's indifference to the *rede*, or council, of the Witan.

The Battle of Hastings. — According to the English "Historical Review" of May, 1894, the English at the Battle of Hastings in 1066 were not protected by a "palisade," and therefore the advance and the feigned flight of the Norman infantry were not for the purpose of forcing this alleged palisade, but solely to tempt the English to break their ranks.

The "Conqueror's" Title. — William I. did not owe his title of the "Conqueror" to this victory. He was, in fact, not transformed into a "conqueror" till some years later — not till all hopes of English freedom had died in the surrender of Ely in 1071. Not even then was he a conqueror in the ordinary sense, for he came only to assert his rights bequeathed to him, as was the custom in those days, by Edward the Confessor.

He did not lay Northern England waste. — The dreadful chastisement following the Northern English resistance to the Normans in 1069, and repeated in every school-book, is undoubtedly an exaggeration. We read that " With fire and sword he [the Conqueror] took a revenge so terrible that from the Humber to the Tyne there stretched for almost a century a vast desolate waste unbroken by the plough." Professor Freeman says, in " The Norman Conquest of England," " The revenge grew in the narratives of later writers into a pitiless laying waste of all Northern England, into a clearance from this region of every form of life. From this representation we may withhold our belief till evidence sufficient to establish so comprehensive a crime be produced."

Rufus was not shot by an Arrow. — The Conqueror's son Rufus — the greedy, the merciless, the irreligious, the hated oppressor of all classes — was not shot accidentally by an arrow from the bow of Walter Tyrrel. He was assassinated. His body bore the marks of three or four sword-thrusts. Almost all the authorities of his time called Tyrrel the " murderer," and the fact that he immediately fled across the sea is strong presumptive evidence. Some authorities opine that his younger brother, Henry, who was in the New Forest at the time, was the instigator of the crime, arguing that William Rufus had despoiled Henry; the Church and barons were suffering from his violent extortions, and longing for speedy relief; the eldest brother, Robert, the rightful heir, was opportunely away in the crusades; Henry, on hearing the news, reached Winchester, in all haste seized the treasure, and put forward the lavish promises that secured him the crown (1100).

Henry I. did not die of Gluttony. — It is commonly said of this Henry that his death was caused by his gluttonous love of lampreys. The accusation is not a just one, because the truth is that the lamprey's skin, like the skin and roe of other fish, is poisonous when eaten at certain times. One may as well bring the charge of gluttony against those suffering through the sometimes deleterious oyster.

The Plantagenets. — The new line of kings beginning with Henry II. (1154) did not know the title under which it is usual to recognize them, the " Plantagenets," a title derived from *planta genesta*, the broom-plant; at least it is not on record that any sovereign ever used that name. It is more correct to style them the Angevins, from Geoffrey [1] of Anjou, the father of the first of this line. He

---

[1] It is doubtful whether this custom of Geoffrey was to indicate a love of field sports, or to show that he was not ashamed to acknowledge the humble founder of the House of Anjou, — a woodman of Rennes, — or to ward off the machinations of witchcraft.

was the only one who is certainly known to have worn a sprig of broom in his cap.

Henry II. did not conceal Fair Rosamond. — There is no truth in the popular legend that says that this king built a labyrinth to conceal his mistress, the " Fair Rosamond " Clifford, from Queen Eleanor, who discovered her by means of a silken thread. The fact is that Henry, instead of concealing her, publicly acknowledged her. Indeed, it would have been quite an extraordinary exception to the State and Church practices of those days to have done otherwise.

Neither was " Fair Rosamond " poisoned by the queen, for she died in the Convent of Godstow, where she long resided as a nun, much esteemed by her companions.

Rosamond was not the Mother of an Archbishop. — Further, Rosamond is commonly, though erroneously, stated to have been the mother of Richard Longsword and Geoffrey, Archbishop of York. Richard was the son of Henry II.; but he was not a Clifford. The argument that he was rests upon a confusion between the Manor of Appleby, in Lincolnshire, which was granted to Longsword by his father, and the Manor of Appleby, in Westmoreland, which was held by Rosamond's family, the Cliffords. Geoffrey, the only non-rebellious one of Henry's children and the only one present at his death-bed, was born of a woman named Hikenai.

A Legend of Becket's Mother. — The mother

of the famous archbishop of this reign — Thomas
Becket — was not of Saracenic origin. The story
goes that a London merchant, while fighting with
the crusaders, was taken prisoner by a Saracen
chieftain, whose daughter fell in love with him; he
escaped and returned to England. The broken-
hearted girl followed, and with the aid of only two
English words, " London " and " Gilbert," reached
London and her lover. But the facts are these:
The archbishop's father, Gilbert Becket, one of the
Norman strangers who followed in the wake of the
Conqueror, was a burgher of Rouen, and his
mother *was of a burgher family* from the neighboring town of Caen.

Bruce and the Spider. — The incident of the
spider connected with the career of Robert the
Bruce is another latter-day fable. Sir Herbert
Maxwell says, in " Robert the Bruce " (" Heroes of
the Nation Series ") : " Where is the evidence to be
found in support of it ? Not in the writings of
Barbour, Fordun, or Wyntoun, those most nearly
contemporary with Bruce, and least likely to sup-
press a circumstance so picturesque and illustrating
so aptly the perseverance and patience of the national hero under desperate difficulties. No; nothing is heard of this adventure till long after Bruce
and his comrades had passed away, and then it
makes its appearance in company with such trash
as the miraculous appearance of the arm bone of
St. Filian on the eve of Bannockburn, and worthy

of just about as much consideration." The same story has been told of another Scottish hero — Sir James Douglas.

Richard Coeur de Léon a Subject of Legend. — In March, 1189, the Emperor Frederick Barbarossa, at Mayence, undertook the third crusade. He died June 10, 1190, as the Christian army was crossing the river Saleph. Richard of England also entered on the crusade, and was present at the capture of Akkon in the autumn of 1191. Leopold V., Duke of Austria, planted his banner on the wall; then went and aided Richard to capture Arsuf, in September, and to restore Joppa. History stops here and fable takes up the dropped thread. It says that Richard tore down the Austrian banner from the palace and flung it into the street; whereat Leopold in anger started home. When Richard, returning in October, 1192, was shipwrecked on the coast of Istria, it is said he dressed as a templar and set out by land. Near Vienna he was betrayed by a gold coin which he chanced to pass, or according to a variant, penetrating to the duke's kitchen, he served as a turnspit and was detected by a costly ring on his finger. In either case, he was arrested and imprisoned, first at Dürenstein, where Blondel de Nesle, the French trouvère, found him by his song. Later, having been transferred to the Emperor Henry VI., he was confined in the Castle of Trivel, where he is said to have won his name of the Lion-hearted by killing a starving lion and eating its heart. Such is the fable.

The truth is this : Richard of England was arrested and delivered to the Emperor, on the ground that he favored the Guelfs, who were the enemies of Henry VI. His appearance in Germany was expected, and spies were set to watch for him.

The secret of his imprisonment was really disclosed by a letter from his captor to Philip of France. Hostages were then found, and the king agreed to remit his own ransom, and did so *after* his return to England, January, 1194. The receipt for it is among the Austrian archives. The popular story does not appear to have been known prior to the fifteenth century.

The French Archer was not flayed Alive. — The offensive story associated with Richard can, however, be traced to its source. Roger of Hovenden — one of the most valued of our early chroniclers, on whom we particularly rely for the events of Richard's reign — states, and the modern histories follow him, that after Richard's death Merchader seized Gourdon, the archer, whose arrow mortally wounded the king before the Castle of Chaluz, flayed him alive, and then hanged him. This is absurd. No medical authority will allow that any one could be flayed *alive*, or that it is possible by the most skilful operation to remove the skin of even half an arm — from the elbow to the wrist — before the patient would die under the shock.

King John did not sign " Magna Charta." — Nelson, on page 123 of his " Royal History," speaking of King John in 1199, says: " And there, with the faintest shadow of objection, John took pen in hand and affixed (*sic*) his royal signature to Magna Charta." A picture accompanying the text represents John actually writing his name with a quill pen. By the way, the Charta is upside down! What the king really did was to affix his seal only, for the very precise reason that he was unable to write.

The early Saxon and Norman kings were content to put their mark, usually a cross, to a document written by a scribe. Not until the reign of Edward III. is a royal sign manual other than a cross placed on a document, the earliest of all being what is described in W. J. Hardy's " Handwritings of the Kings and Queens of England " as words equivalent to his signature by the Black Prince. The words in question are *Homout Ich Dene* on a writ of 1370. But the Charta was signed, *i.e.*, sealed, in 1215.

Recent fac-similes of the Great Charter have been copied, as the publishers state, by " express permission from the original document in the British Museum." Mr. C. E. Clarke availed himself of an " express permission," and found, instead of an original document, only a few square inches of charred parchment rescued from the fire of 1731, and tenderly cemented on what is, perhaps, cardboard.

One detail of the fac-simile was the entire red seal hanging on a cord; whereas the original has only half a seal, in brown — not red — wax, hanging on a strip of curled parchment.

The Garter on another Footing. — The ordinarily accepted story of the founding of the Order of the Garter is a legend. It states that the beautiful Countess of Salisbury, while dancing, lost the blue garter from her left leg. King Edward III. threw himself at her feet, picked up the precious object, and in order to stifle the sarcasms that might and perhaps did go from mouth to mouth, he uttered the famous phrase *honny soit qui mal y pense* ("evil to him who evil thinks") and founded the exclusive society which has that motto.

Another legend, less authenticated, but regarded as more probable, has it that King Edward at the battle of Crécy, in 1346, gave the signal of attack by elevating a garter on the end of his lance, with the battle-cry "St. George," and in remembrance of his victory over Philippe de Valois founded the order, giving its device to guard against criticism of the name. The motto was known in the Middle Ages.

Neither of these legends is known to the order itself. The statutes state that Edward founded it "to the glory of God, the Blessed Virgin, and the

Holy Martyr St. George, the Protector of England, in the twenty-third year of his reign."

The First Prince of Wales. — In 1301, in the next reign but one, that of Edward I., the greatest of the "Plantagenets," the first Prince of Wales, and weakest of the "Plantagenets," received his title; but the chamber in Carnarvon Castle, shown as his birthplace, is an imaginary shrine. It has been proved beyond doubt by the well-known archæologist, Mr. Albert Hartshorne, that the castle was barely begun by Edward I., and not finished till thirty-three years after the babyhood of this his fourth son.

Queen Eleanor and the Fable of the Poison. — Neither did Queen Eleanor, the mother of this boy, suck the poison from the arm of his father, as she did not accompany the king on his Palestine expedition, 1270–72, during which this incident is alleged to have taken place.

The Prince of Wales' Three Feathers. — The grandson of this first Prince of Wales "won his spurs" near the forest of Crécy, 1346. At the battle John, the blind King of Bohemia, was among the slain, and his crest is supposed to have become the possession of the Black Prince, and to have ever since been borne by the Princes of Wales. This crest is almost universally believed to have consisted of three ostrich feathers. But John's seal, still extant, shows there were not three, but nearer fifty, and the feathers were not from the ostrich,

but from the eagle; and, further, that the feathers
were not arranged like our familiar designs, but like
a widely opened feather fan, extending over the top
of the helmet to the back in much the same way as
a Red Indian wears his feathers.[1]

It is suggested that the three plumes in the modern crest were originally not feathers at all, but
fleurs-de-lis; and also that only John's motto, " I
serve " (*Ich dien*), was assumed and transferred to
the arms of France by the Black Prince to empha-
size that, whereas formerly the objective of " I
serve " was the French king, it now meant, in token
of victory, " I serve (and the *fleurs-de-lis* with me)
the English king, my father (Edward III.)."

The Fleur-de-Lis. — On Assyrian monuments
date-trees are always figured with ibex or goats'
horns tied to the trees to ward off the mischief of the
evil eye.   It is done in Sicily and Southern Italy at
the present day.   The device was taken up by the
Greeks, and what is known as the honeysuckle pat-
tern is nothing but ibex horns tied to a tree.   The
crusaders in the East took this to be a royal emblem and brought it home to France, where it was
adopted as the *fleur-de-lis.*

The Black Prince did not always wear Black.
— The Black Prince, says the author of " Names
and Their Meaning," " was not exclusively addicted
to the wearing of black armor, as he is usually

---

[1] P. Norman, in " London Signs and Inscriptions," 1893, says:
" King John's crest was a vulture's wing expanded."

represented in waxwork shows and picture toy-books; consequently he did not derive his name from such an association." As the useful, though not always trustworthy, Froissart informs us, " He received his name by terror of his arms." The helmet and coat of mail hanging over the prince's tomb in Canterbury Cathedral bear no evidence of ever having been black.

Why Wat Tyler was killed. — Thirty-one years after Crécy the Black Prince's son was crowned as Richard II.; four years later the Peasants' Revolt occurred, and its leader, Wat Tyler, was killed at Smithfield by one of the king's esquires, Walworth, — Mayor of London — not as an insurgent, but for having set fire to all the Southwark houses of ill-fame which the Mayor held as a very profitable monopoly.

How did Richard II. die? — When Shakespeare, in " Richard II.," follows the story commonly current as to the death of Richard II., and makes Sir Pierce of Exton murder him at Pomfret, we are rightly sympathetic, but when school histories do the same they pervert facts. An English text-book says: " The dethroned king died in the dungeons of Pontefract, either by starvation or by the hand of an assassin."

This is worded and accepted as if it were a correct statement. Other accounts with equal emphasis assert that it was a case of suicide.

But the truth is that after Richard's abdication he

entirely disappears from history; neither the time of his death is known for certain, nor that it took place at Pomfret; and there is no evidence to prove that Richard died other than a natural death.

Another of Shakespeare's Lies.—The "Madcap" son who caused so much anxiety to Henry IV. during his declining years, and who was about twelve years of age when Chaucer died, was not sent to prison by Sir William Gascoigne, the judge, for striking him while on the Bench, nor was Gascoigne reappointed by the prince when he became Henry V. The story did not appear for a hundred and fifty years after that time; and the tradition is mainly kept afloat by Shakespeare's " Henry IV." (second part), Act V., Scene II.

The City of London Arms. — The dagger in the City of London Arms is generally supposed to have been granted by Richard to Sir William Walworth for his assistance in putting down the Kentish iron-founders' rebellion. This is not true, for " it had been there long before, and perhaps referred to past services of the citizens in furnishing arms; or, more likely, to St. Paul, the city's patron saint, whose emblem it was."

Dick Whittington had no Cat.—In 1397, during the reign of Henry IV., the famous Dick Whittington was Lord Mayor of London. But the old legend which depicts him as going to London and achieving his fortune by means of his cat is not true. An Eastern legend of the same nature is the

origin of the whole tale. The phrase "Whittington and his cat" is supposed to be made from the
French word *achat*, used in the 14th century to designate buying or selling at a profit, and probably
pronounced in English "acat," and then simply
"cat." When its meaning had been almost forgotten, some inventive genius found the disused word a
very convenient stock on which to graft the Eastern
story.

According to tradition, Whittington made his
"cat" by trading in coals, which were first made an
article of trade from Newcastle to London in 1381.

Jack Cade was a Gentleman. — At the death
of Whittington the new king, Henry VI., was but
fifteen months old, and some twenty-seven years
later the well-organized gathering from Kent, Sur-
rey, and Sussex, known as the Jack Cade Rebellion,
assembled on Blackheath, and after retracing their
steps to Sevenoaks, where they routed the king's
forces, marched to London, which, by a vote of ad-
mittance from the Common Council, they occupied
for some days.

The "Captain of Kent," as the leader called
himself, was not a wanton Socialist and the illiter-
ate person and impostor that Shakespeare so completely caricatured in "Henry VI." (second part).

On the contrary, he was, in a political sense, a
humane reformer, with a well-defined program
based on a cause as just as that which secured
Magna Charta. He had served with distinction in

the French wars, and owned land — both freehold and leasehold — in Kent. His enterprise was arranged strictly under the regular local machinery and was backed by many of the squires of Kent and adjoining counties, as well as by some prominent Churchmen — the great landowners, Abbot of Battle and Prior of Lewes.

The "Complaint of the Commons of Kent" ably set forth the grievances of the people and their demands, — economy of public money, exactions under color of law, and freedom of election, — and Cade enforced it with dignity, tact, and courage; but the Fates, with Shakespeare and school histories, have combined to give him the libellous character of an unruly impostor and a vulgarly impudent rebel, who undertook to make himself king and "to sell seven half-penny loaves for a penny."

Sebastian Cabot did not discover the American Continent. — Sebastian Cabot is sometimes still mentioned as the discoverer of North America. The Sebastian thesis was undermined years since, and exploded a little later by Mr. Weare, whose account of the Cabot voyages is most complete. Though in Henry VII.'s Letters Patent Sebastian is mentioned with his father, John Cabot, it is certain that he did not accompany him in the voyage of 1497, that in which the continent was discovered. It is equally certain that he was not a member of the second expedition, from which John

Cabot never returned.   " The undoubted discoverer was the never-to-be-forgotten John Cabot."

The Duke of Clarence was not drowned in Wine. — Edward in 1477 impeached his brother, the Duke of Clarence, who was thereupon condemned to die within the Traitor's Gate, and was there secretly made away with. There is, however, absolutely no evidence to show that the duke was drowned in a butt of Malmsey wine, either in the dark, windowless room pointed out in the Bloody Tower or anywhere else.

The Traitor's Gate shown to visitors at the Tower of London is not the original (which Phineas Barnum told G. A. Sala he had purchased at a sale of condemned government stores, and which he intended to erect at the entrance to his New York museum), but a " modernized sham."

What really happened to Jane Shore. — A 17th century ballad entitled, " The Woful Lamentations of Jane Shore, a Goldsmith's Wife in London, sometime King Edward IV. his Concubine," says:

> " I yielded up my vital strength
> Within a ditch of loathsome scent,
> Where carrion dogs did much frequent."

The tale that Jane Shore, worn out with agonizing poverty and hunger, and discarded by the king, died miserably in a ditch is wholly erroneous.

Jane Shore survived Edward by thirty years, and

died at a ripe old age in a religious house. Her penance at St. Paul's, maliciously ordered by Richard III., is alluded to by Michael Drayton. In spite of this order, which extended to the robbing of her house as well, poverty was averted by the care of the Marquis of Dorset. In the reign of Henry VIII. Sir Thomas More distinctly asserts that she was then alive, and seems to imply that he himself had seen her.

Jane did not give her Name to Shoreditch. — Shoreditch, as a matter of fact, took its name from the old family of the Soerdiches, who were lords of the manor in the time of Edward III. Stowe mentions a house at Hackney called Shoreditch Place, probably the old mansion of Sir John Soerdiche, who was one of the brothers-in-arms with the Black Prince.

Richard III. not a Humpback. — Richard III. may have been a monster of iniquity, as Sir Thomas More and other Tudor partisans describe him, yet he was no worse than his brother, and certainly he was less unscrupulous than his successor; but to call him "ugly" and a "hunchback," because Shakespeare does, is unjust.

Besides possessing great muscular strength, a pleasant if not handsome face, and desperate courage, he had the perfect figure of a soldier.

Bloody Queen Mary. — The evils with which popular opinion has stained the character of Queen Mary were really perpetrated through the instigations and under the direction of the Archbishop of Canterbury, Cardinal Pole, and the Spanish Court then residing in England, after the marriage between Mary and Philip of Spain. He alone, if anybody, should in strictness bear the dishonorable distinction.

The full extent of the sanguinary persecutions of her short reign was hardly known to her — for during a great part of the time she was in a state of deep depression and inactivity, owing to mental and bodily ill-health. It has not been proved that her disposition was cruel and harsh.

Edward VI. was not a Founder of Schools. — Mr. Leache's learned "English Schools of the Reformation" shows conclusively that Edward VI., instead of being a great founder of schools, had been their great spoiler, some three hundred being suppressed under him and his father. "Never was a great reputation so easily gained and less deserved than that of King Edward VI. as a founder of schools."

But it should be remembered that "Edward VI." stands for his Council, not "the poor, rickety, over-educated boy, who was only sixteen when he died," and who, with the very doubtful exception of Christ's Hospital, had personally no lot in the matter.

Edward's government must be considered as not having founded a single school. At the death of the Protector Somerset, the Duke of Northumberland managed to induce the Council to reëndow a few of those schools that had been robbed; but that was all.

The Pilgrim Fathers. — The Pilgrim Fathers of the days of James I. did not emigrate straight away from England to America, as many suppose. The little band of Lincolnshire "Puritans" at first fled to Leyden in Holland, and some years later departed for Delft, where, after a farewell prayer-meeting in the church, they embarked for New England, or rather for the Hudson, calling for friends at Southampton on their way. There is an absurd idea that the Pilgrim Fathers of popular fame differed widely in their views from the men of the "Mayflower." Puritanism arose in the reign of Queen Elizabeth, and the sect split into two or more branches, of which the Pilgrims, who were Separatists, having openly withdrawn from the National Church and practised the prerogative of self-rule, formed one, founding the Brownist or Congregational Church, but the Puritans were strict Church of England men, and so were the Massachusetts colonists. Thus Francis Higginson, who came to Salem in 1629, remarked, "We do not go to New England as Separatists from the Church of England, though we cannot but separate from the corruptions in it; but we go to practise the positive part of church reformation;" and Winthrop's company spoke of the Church of England as their "dear Mother." You will see "Pilgrim Fathers" defined

as the name given to one hundred and two Puritans
who sailed in the "Mayflower" from Plymouth.
Pilgrim and Puritan are not the same; the Pilgrim
Fathers did not start from Plymouth. It may be
of some interest to mention that in the vestibule of
the House of Lords is a fine painting, by Cope, of
the sailing of the "Mayflower." It was formerly
inscribed, "Departure of a Puritan Family for New
England." Lords Macaulay and Stanhope gave a
hearing to the artist and others interested; and
seeing their habitual error in confounding Puritan
with Separatist, they, as Commissioners on Decora-
tions, changed "A Puritan Family" to "Pilgrim
Fathers."

The Puritans were not so Strict. — The idea
prevalent is that Cromwellian Puritanism signifies
the bigotry of "gloomy fanatics." That it was another name for dulness consequent upon the assump-
tion of a too elevated standard of moral conduct is
proved by the enthusiasm with which Charles II.
was welcomed back to the throne. But to suppose
that the Puritans were harsh and sour and tried to
crush out all forms of pleasure and amusement is a
great mistake.

Cromwell was fond of out-door games and sport,
and liked horses, although it is not true that he ever
kept race-horses.

We find that the benchers of the Middle Temple
gave a great dance in their hall in 1651, and the
additional fact that the exercise was inaugurated by

singing a psalm eloquently declares the ideal of Puritanism to be not in the present debased meaning of the word "Puritanical," but rather of God-fearing restraint.

Moreover, magnificent State dinners were accompanied by music, which was an innovation at that time, and Sabbatarians will be horrified when they discover that Cromwell opened his last Parliament on Sunday with a magnificent ceremonial. "The better the day the better the deed" was obviously Cromwell's maxim.

Cromwell and Hampden did not attempt to sail to America just before the outbreak of the English revolution. A number of their friends did, but they had no thought of going.

The Execution of Charles I. — The conventional conception of the historic scene at Whitehall (Jan. 30, 1649) when Charles I. was executed shows him kneeling down and laying his head upon a block several feet high. Such is the one preserved at the Tower as the original block on which Lord Kilmarnock and Lord Balmerino were executed, the one in 1746, the other in 1747.

This is a mistake. There was no such block, and Charles did not kneel. He simply lay flat at full length on the scaffold, and his head was cut off as it lay over a little piece of wood not more than two or three inches high. Among so many who suffered in this way was Lady Jane Grey

(1554), and therefore not on the Tower block, as is often supposed.

There is ample proof that the method of beheading in Tudor and Cromwellian times necessitated the victim lying prone on the scaffold. John Button's "Descriptive Sketches of Tunbridge Wells" declares that Judge Jeffreys presided over the trial of King Charles I.

The Tree Charles did not hide in. — The dance in which the Puritans took part celebrated the scattering of Charles II.'s army at Worcester (1651), and hundreds of pious tourists every year visit Boscobel Oak, which is reputed to possess the distinction of having concealed Charles for a whole day after the battle, while he watched through its leafy screen Oliver's soldiers searching for him. Scientific evidence shows that the tree, being only eleven feet ten inches in girth, could not have been the pollard oak of nearly two and a half centuries ago.

In 1817 an inscription, afterwards removed, expressly intimated "the present tree" to have sprung from the royal oak. It has been ascertained that the original tree, whether deserving of the celebrity attaching to it or not, disappeared soon after 1787, the oak long before that date having been almost cut away by relic hunters who came to see it.

Boys and others gather oak leaves on the 29th of May to commemorate the king's mode of concealment. But the king hid himself early in September. Had he climbed an oak-tree in May, the foliage would not have been sufficiently developed to conceal him. What is really celebrated, and, perhaps, combined with the former event, is his restoration in 1660, when his route through London was strewn with oak branches.

Nelson did not disobey Parker. — Only about eleven months before Dr. Jenner's fame had reached its zenith, Lord Nelson returned to England after his " glorious *disobedience* " at Copenhagen (1801). We all know the story — so often repeated to characterize Nelson's reckless and determined bravery — of Nelson putting his telescope to his sightless eye and declaring that he did not see Sir Hyde Parker's signal to discontinue fighting. But Prof. Knox Laughton explains away this story and substitutes phenomenal coolness for reckless disobedience. He says: " It is very well established that Parker sent his flag-captain, Otway, with a verbal message that the signal was to be understood as permissive, and was made in that way so that the whole responsibility might rest with Parker, if Nelson judged it advisable to discontinue the action. If he thought it advisable to continue it he was at liberty to do so. He judged it right to continue; and the little pantomime was only a joke, at the expense of Colonel Stewart standing by, who had no knowledge of the message Otway had brought."

The Massacre of Glencoe not by Englishmen. — The Highlanders joyfully believed that the restoration had permanently secured the ancient name of Stewart, but the Massacre of Glencoe in 1692 dashed their hopes. Thousands believe that the Macdonalds were massacred by a party of English soldiers, in consequence of an order signed by William III. The truth is that neither the instigators nor the assassins were Englishmen; they were all inhabitants of Scotland, and neighbors — and some were relatives — of the murdered men.

" The king signed this warrant under the impression that the Macdonalds of Glencoe were the main obstacles to the pacification of the Highlands, the fact that Macdonald had submitted being carefully kept from his knowledge. The iniquitous act was done at the instigation of the Earl of Braedalbane, whose lands had been plundered during the late hostilities by the men of Glencoe, and who thirsted for vengeance on that account, and also because his treachery to William had been exposed by Macdonald himself, who showed that he had been secretly negotiating with the other clans. The execution of the warrant of extermination was therefore urged on by the Secretary of State (the friend of Braedalbane) with the utmost rigor." The full facts can be read by any one in " Notes to the Highland Widow," by Sir W. Scott.

Her Majesty is not a Guelph. — Queen Victoria and the other members of the Houses of Brunswick-

Lüneberg and Hanover are descended from Azon,
Margrave of Este. Her name and that of the Duke
of Cumberland who claimed the throne of Hanover
is Azon, or Azon von Este. The Prince of Wales,
being the son of Albert of Saxe-Coburg, is neither
a Guelph nor an Azon; he belongs to the Wettin
line, which was founded by the first Count of Wettin
in the twelfth century. The Queen's given names
are Alexandrina Victoria, and her partiality for the
second, and as it were inferior, name arises from the
fact that it was her mother's. The first name commemorates her godfather, the Emperor of Russia.

Tsar Nicholas is an Oldenburg. — The Emperor of Russia is known as a Románof, but if
instead of tracing his descent through the feminine
line we trace his name to the father of his race, in
accordance with the generally accepted rule, it is
found to be Oldenburg. For the same reason, it is
not correct to call the members of the English
Royal family Guelphs.

Mistaken Anniversaries. — In " Peveril of the
Peak" and several other books the 17th of November is spoken of as the anniversary of the birth of
Queen Elizabeth. She was born on the 7th of September, 1533, and the 17th of November was the
anniversary of her accession in 1558, and consequently was " the birthday of the Protestant religion."

In the same way the accession of Queen Victoria,
June 20, has been recently confounded with her

coronation, which took place on the 23d of September.

About the Armada. — For three centuries the failure of the great Spanish Armada has been popularly believed to have been due to its dissipation by a great storm. The legend struck off at the time was, "*Flavit Deus et dissipati sunt.*" From a religious point of view such a representation is childish; from the historical it is false.

The Spanish fleet had already met with a crushing defeat in which the English had destroyed many ships and men before it was overtaken by storms in the Northern seas. That fleet was badly commanded, badly equipped. The best English seamen did not believe in the seaworthiness of the Spanish vessels, which were overmasted and leaking.

By August 4th five of the most important Spanish ships had not a drop of water; very little food was on hand, and many of the men were ill. It is doubtful whether 120 Spanish ships of all sizes came into the channel, while the total number of Spanish fighting men was not more than from 10,000 to 12,000. (Green's "History" says: "Spain had 149 ships and 28,000 men.")

On the other hand, England had 197 ships and about 18,000 men. (Green says: "Only 80 ships and 9,000 men.") The English sailors also were accustomed to the great open seas, while the Spaniards were mainly fair-weather seamen. Thus it will be seen that the defeat of the Armada, like the recent defeat at Sant' Iago and Manila, was due, not to storms, still less to Divine favoritism, but to the simple fact that England had the better navy.[1]

Why the Armada was sent. — The reason for sending this great expedition against England was Mary Queen of Scots' transference of her interest in the English succession to Philip, for this was made after the Armada had been projected; not the pressing need of destroying Protestantism, nor Elizabeth's refusal to marry Philip, — yet each of these motives may be found advocated in various text-books as explanatory of "Castile's black fleet."

We must understand that the Anglo-Spanish conflict began several years before the Armada appeared, and also that its immediate cause was not the dislike of the Inquisition, but the dread of a hostile power establishing itself in the seaports of the Netherlands, and the special fear by English statesmen that France would join Spain in making the attempt, in which case the history of British progress might have been considerably delayed.

An English army was, therefore, sent there, and miserably failed; but the English fleet swept the Spanish West Indies, — where "an exclusive com-

---

[1] How closely the facts and figures agree with those given by Mr. Hume — the acknowledged authority on the Elizabethan period — may be seen in the "Nineteenth Century" for September, 1897.

mercial policy, adopted and enforced by the Spanish Government," led Hawkins, Drake, and others into smuggling and bloody reprisals, — and it was the naval success of England in her illicit traffic with the Spanish colonies that determined Philip on the expedition of the Armada.

During the alarm of the Spanish invasion the command of the land forces was intrusted to the Earl of Leicester — the courtier who intrigued to obtain the favor of his peers in proposing marriage with the queen, and who, in the interests of which project, is supposed to have procured the murder of his wife, Amy Robsart.

Rizzio's Bloodstains. — Six years after Amy's murder the blood of Rizzio, the Italian Secretary of Mary Stuart, was shed on the floor of Holyrood by certain Protestant leaders, aided by the queen's husband, Darnley, and in the imagination of the public the stain has not yet disappeared. But what is seen there is not Rizzio's blood. It may have been at one time a daub of red paint; perhaps pig's blood — any suggestion will do. The stain — assuming of course that it is over three hundred years old — may be the blood of one of the *conspirators*, for "so eager and reckless were they in their ferocity that in the struggle to get at him *they wounded one another*." But then why are there not *many* stains? All the guide-books speak of *a certain* stain. Surely fifty-six stabs would have been sufficient to deluge the place. By what inherent virtue is this *certain* stain alone able to remain? Simply, we repeat, because it is painted and renewed with a superstition, still prevalent, that bloodstains cannot be washed out.

Queen Mary's Bed. — Of equal consequence to the confiding sightseer, no less than to his guide's frame of mind, are the well-attested disclosures that "Queen Mary's bed, also at Holyrood, is of the last century, and her room at Hardwick is in a house which was not erected till after her death," at Fotheringay, in 1587.

CHAPTER XI.

CURIOUS BLUNDERS IN GENERAL HISTORY.

Mediæval Dirt. — The Right Hon. Dr. Lyon Playfair, M.P. (pronounced Pluffer), stated in an address delivered at Glasgow in October, 1874, that " for a thousand years there was not a man or woman in Europe that ever took a bath ! " And he attributes to the extraordinary condition of things the epidemics that ravaged the Middle Ages. Michelet before him said the same thing. It is probably a gross libel on our ancestors. Viollet-le-Duc states that in the twelfth century bath-rooms were built in houses as now, only they were more commodious than ours.

Moguls and Romans. — Speaking of the Mogul Empire, Freeman [1] says : " This dynasty is commonly known as Mogul, both in and out of India ; but Baber " — who founded the so-called Mogul Empire in 1525–26 — " was for all practical purposes a Turk. His memoirs were written in Turkish ; and he always speaks of the real Moguls with dislike. The cause of the misnomer is that the name Mogul is in India loosely applied to all

[1] " History of the Saracens," p. 292.

strangers from the North, much in the same way
as that of Turk is throughout the East for all
strangers from the West.   It is even applied to the
Persians with hardly more reason than the Persians
themselves have for calling the Ottoman Turks
Romans."

The Eastern Empire, being the legitimate successor of the Holy Roman Empire, was known to
the Mediæval Persians as Rûm.   When the Ottoman Turks succeeded in capturing Constantinople
or Byzantium, the name Rûm was still loosely
applied to all that region.   So it is hardly true to
state that the Persians call the Turks Romans.

William Tell did not exist. — Until 1836 it
was believed that the story of Wilhelm Tell in all
its poetic details was an historic fact.   But in that
year a German named Bopp subjected the legend
to a rigid examination and separated its historic
foundations from fable.   The first attempt of the
Swiss to throw off the yoke of the Habsburgs was
in 1231, when the canton of Uri was freed from
Count Rudolf.   Schwyz followed in 1240, and
some years later Unterwalden obtained the same
boon.   In 1291, the year of the death of the Emperor Rudolf I., Niedwalden and Oberwalden
joined forces.   On August 1 the three first can-
tons made a defensive alliance.   Open war broke
out shortly after between the Swiss and Austria,
and lasted till 1293, when Albrecht, Rudolf's son,
made peace.   This lasted with various interrup-

tions till into the fifteenth century. The battle of Morgarten on the 16th of November, 1315, when an insignificant horde of shepherds and peasants won a brilliant victory over the best-trained troops and ablest generals of Austria, was the foundation-stone of the famous Bund der Eidgenossen. In the oldest chronicle, that of the monk Johannes von Winterthür (1340–1347), which describes the battle of Morgarten, nothing is said of Tell, Staufacher, Melchtal, Fürst, or of Gessler and Landenberg. Nor in any other account of these circumstances is there any hint of the legend until 1470, when the so-called " White Book " was published. In this the story is told in simple form, and the scene of the Rütlibund is laid in Unter-walden. Melchior Russ, of Lucerne, in his chronicle of 1482, makes Tell the leader, but lays the scene in Uri. But there are no conspirators and no Rüt-libund. Elterlin, in the sixteenth century, and Stumpf, in 1548, call the Landvogt Grissler; and Stumpf dates the conspiracy 1313, after the death of the Emperor Heinrich. The famous Swiss chronicler Tschudi, of Glarus, who died in 1572, gave its present form to the story; but certain details — that Tell was from Burglen, that he was Walter Fürst's son-in-law, and that he had two sons, Walter and Wilhelm, that Gessler's name was Hermann, or that the conspiracy was called Rütli — were left for Johannes Müller, at the end of the last century, to add; and Müller obtained them from the pious priests who invented them.

Tell, then, is a myth made up of folk legends common to many peoples and lands. The story is told, in a ballad, about the archer William of Cloudesley, and in legendary history as occurring even in English territory: "The canton of Schwyz, in August, 1890, ordered the story of Tell to be expunged (as being non-historical and legendary only) from the school-books of the canton." The London "Echo" for May 23d is authority for the statement that in Scotland Tell's name was Leod; in Scandinavia, Palmatoke; in Denmark, Tako. Also in Persia the Tell myth was popular. There was a Landvogt named Gessler in 1386 at Thurgam, and a knight Ulrich Gessler in 1369 at Meyenberg.

The Story of Arnold von Winkelried is a Legend. — Poetry has enjoyed great license with the story of the heroic Winkelried. In the oldest chronicle of the battle of Sempach, written by Justinger, the city scribe of Bern, not a word is said of Winkelried, or of the Wall of Lances. In one of the Zürich chronicles it says: "After the Confederates had suffered great losses, God helped them to the victory. This was due to a true man among the Confederates. When he saw that things were going so ill with his comrades, and that the gentlemen were everywhere piercing the foremost in the ranks with their lances and pikes before the Swiss could reach them with their halberds, this honorable, pious man pushed forward and seized as many pikes as he could grasp and bore them down so that the Confederates could now push forward. And with joy he shouted: "All in the rear are in flight!" "*So fliehen Alle da hinten!*"

The name of the hero is not given nor is his death mentioned. His rejoicing in the flight of the enemy would seem to disprove that he was killed. But the whole story is an addendum inserted ten years after the chronicle was composed and eighty years after the battle. Melchior Russ, who wrote in 1486, a hundred years after the battle, knew nothing of the circumstance. Winkelried's name was not heard of before the sixteenth century, and the same Tschudi who did so much to formulate the Tell myth was the inventor of the name of this hero — a name, however, well known in Switzerland in other connections.

Who invented the Art of Printing? — Many persons suppose that Gutenberg knew only the art of printing from wooden types, and that Peter Schöffer was the first to make steel matrixes, and thus deserves the credit of being its inventor. Gutenberg was a metal worker and goldsmith; and he it was who invented the art of printing from metallic types in 1450. The credit was stolen from him by his unscrupulous assistant, Johann Fust or Faust, and was afterwards by some attributed to his son-in-law, Peter Schöffer.

The Printing-press. — The death of Henry VI. and the ascendency of the House of York (Edward IV., 1461) bring us, within a few years, to the most serviceable agency in the evolution of social England — the introduction of the printing press. Faulty text-books have it that the earliest book printed in England was "The Game and Playe of the Chesse," and that this book was printed in Westminster "Abbey" in 1474.

It was translated from the French in that year, and, although published the following year in England, was *printed* in Bruges. Moreover, Caxton did not set up his printing-plant until 1476, and it was near, not inside, but outside, the church ; Green says "in the almonry, a little enclosure containing the almshouses, near the west front." The first book actually printed in England was Caxton's "Dictes or Sayinges of the Philosophers," which was completed in November of the year 1477.

Columbus' Egg a Myth. — Benzoni, in his "History of the New World" (1565), is said to have been the first to tell the story of Columbus standing the egg on end. It is quoted with approval by Washington Irving, and Mr. Clements R. Markham, in his "Columbus" (1897), says : "Although it was first told fifty years after the admiral's death, it may quite possibly be founded on fact." It is now known to have been Brunelleschi, the architect, and not Columbus, who stood an egg on end, and he did it in the simple way of the story, so as to silence critics, who asked him how he was going to support the dome of Sante Maria dei Fiori, the cathedral of Florence.

Columbus was not Columbus. — There is also some misunderstanding associated with the name of the Great Discoverer. Columbus was not his paternal name any more than it was " Plantagenet."

It was only a borrowed title — a sea term that covered up some early mystery of his birth. It was a name acquired from two pirates, or corsairs, father and son, known by the merchants whom they chased as the Columbi, from their flag, which depicted a dove, *colombo*.

The great Columbus sailed under their flag, claimed them as his relatives, and fought and plundered with them on the high seas. So great was the terror inspired by the merciless sea-rovers that the very name alone was a guarantee of non-resistance. How unlikely, then, the use of a less famous one, or that the world would use that one regarding which Columbus himself has always preserved silence!

Washington Irving and the Monks of Newstead. — In 1780 the lake near Newstead Abbey was drained and deepened, and the workmen found a large brass bookstand which had once belonged to the monks. It was shaped like an eagle, and had been thrown in the lake at the dissolution of the monastery in 1536. The globe on which the eagle stood was found to be full of documents, and Wash-

ington Irving in his book on Newstead states that
the parchments threw an awkward light on the
monks. Byron sneers also at the bold immorality
of the " holy men " who once lived there. But later
examination proves that the document was only a
general pardon forced on religious houses by Henry
V., and had nothing to do with the morals of
Newstead.

The Borgias.— There is very good reason to
believe that Alexander VI. was a worthy pope and
a great king, that Cesare Borgia was the defender
of the liberty of his people, and that Lucrezia Borgia,
far from being the modern Messalina, was a pure
and lovable woman ; that the stories about the
crimes of the Borgias are inventions and calumnies.

Max Piccolomini no Myth.— In Schiller's
splendid trilogy " Wallenstein " Max Piccolomini is
represented as the son of the field marshal Ottavio
Piccolomini and in love with Thekla, the daughter
of Wallenstein. But it has been shown that Ottavio
Piccolomini was married only five years previous to
his death, and Thekla Wallenstein was fourteen in
1634. It is true, however, that Ottavio Piccolomini
had in his household a nephew named Joseph Sylvio
whom he dearly loved, and who was killed in a
battle with the Swedes in March, 1645.

Don Carlos died a Natural Death.— The drama
and the muse of history have found rich material
for imagination in the story of Don Carlos, the
second son of King Philip II. of Spain. Many his-

tories state that he was executed by command of his father, and Schiller's famous tragedy turns on this incident. It is now well proved by historical documents that as the infanta, who had expressed deep hatred of his father, was on the point of fleeing from Spain, he was arrested on the night of Jan. 18–19, 1568, and died unexpectedly, but by a natural death, in prison at one o'clock on the morning of July 23 of the same year. The story soon spread that he had been executed, and that Philip II. had also caused his queen, Elizabeth of Valois, to be poisoned. She died October 3. But the story that she had had illicit relations with the young man was a gross libel.

The Age of Champagne. — It is generally supposed that champagne is an entirely modern wine. Brillot-Savarin states in his "Philology of Taste" that it was first known in the fourteenth century. There is an apocryphal story to the effect that Charles VI. of France gave a feast at Rheims in May, 1397, to the Roman Emperor and King Wenceslaus of Bohemia, who were so pleased with this new wine that they and their followers could not drink enough of it in a month of steady drinking. But bottles were not generally used till the last century, and "corkage" was an unknown factor. The first cork was used by Pérignon, cellarer to the Abbey of Haute Villers in the eighteenth century. Champagne is said to be first mentioned in print in 1718, coupled with the statement that it had been known for twenty years.

The Story of the Iron Mask. — The history of the mysterious man in the iron (or properly the velvet) mask excited the curiosity of Europe for nearly two hundred years. It was rumored that he was a natural son of Louis XIV., who having been incarcerated in 1660, a month after the death of Mazarin, was kept at the Bastille until his death in 1703, when, according to Voltaire, he was secretly buried in the graveyard of St. Paul's Church. After his death every document relating to him was supposed to have been burnt; the walls whitewashed and the floors torn up, that no trace of his existence might remain. During the eighteenth century no less than eight persons were identified with this prisoner; among them the Duc de Beaufort whom Dumas pictures in prison in "Vingt Ans Après," but who really died at the Turkish assault in Candia, June 26, 1669; Henry Cromwell, second son of the Protector; the Duke of Monmouth, natural son of King Charles II.; an Armenian patriarch; Ercole Matioli, minister to the Duke of Mantua, who was said to have sworn to betray to Louis XIV. the castle of Casale, but proved recreant to his word.

Benché tried to make out that the story was a legend, but in 1873 a book was published in Paris giving substantial reasons for believing that the man in the iron mask was Harmoises, a noble of Lorraine, who put himself at the head of a conspiracy against Louis XIV. He was arrested March

19, 1673, and confined in various prisons, dying finally at the Bastille.

Louis Philippe no Changeling. — Dr. Hugh Macmillan, in his " Gate Beautiful," asserts that " Louis Philippe had all the low tastes and cowardly feelings of the ignoble race to which he is said to have belonged, though seated on the throne of France; whereas the real child of the French king, who was supposed to have been exchanged for him when he was born because she was a girl, exhibited all the pride and dauntless courage of the Bourbons in her humble condition." The girl who claimed to be daughter of the Duc d'Orléans (Égalité) was Maria Stella Petronilla, putative daughter of an Italian, Crappini. She was married first to the earl of Newborough and secondly to Baron Sternberg, and the tribunal of Faenza recognized her claims. But the story was wholly a fabrication. Louis Philippe's father was also said to be the bastard son of Louis, Comte de Melfort.

Charlotte d'Éon de Beaumont was a Man. — The story once widely believed that the Chevalier d'Éon was a woman is a complete fable. The man who bore the feminine names of Charlotte, Geneviève, Louise, Auguste, was born at Tonnerre in Burgundy, and served in the Seven Years' War as Captain of Dragoons and Aide to Marshal Broglio; afterwards as secretary of Legation in London. He certainly in later life wore the dress of a woman — it is said by command of Louis XVI., who desired him thus to hide certain indiscretions. After the outbreak of the Revolution, 1791, he petitioned the National Assembly from England to be allowed to resume his rank in the army. But his petition was disregarded; his pension was taken from him and he was obliged to sell his library. As late as 1809 it was still believed by men in authority that he was a woman, and not till after his death, May 10, 1810, was the contrary definitely established.

Moscow was not set on fire by the Russians. — Moscow was not destroyed by the Russians; its destruction was due to the negligence of the French soldiers when smoking, and to their rough cooking arrangements. In a town built chiefly of wood, where fires were of every-day occurrence in spite of the vigilance of police and landlords, the catastrophe was inevitable when those care-takers fled and when the French had, of course, not thought of organizing precautions.

A legend that has been accepted as truth for eighty years cannot, however, be overthrown by mere deductions, so Count Tolstoï produces proof in the shape of letters written by the very men who are said to have been the patriotic authors of the fire. Among these alleged incendiaries stands preëminently Count Rostopchin. He wrote to the Emperor Alexander to inform him that on the 2d of December fires had broken out in the ware-houses and corn-stores all along the wall of the Kremlin, and he was then in doubt whether they were the work of the invaders or of their owners.

A few days later he again wrote to Alexander accusing Napoleon of the act, and concluding with the remark that if he had known two or three days previously what was about to happen, he himself would have set fire to the city, in order to have deprived Napoleon " of the glory of saying that he took Moscow and sacked and burnt it."

Coronation Mugs. — The historic coronation mugs that were distributed to the crowds in May, 1897, at Moscow were not of Russian manufacture, but came from Vienna. The curious craze of the populace to obtain them resulted from a rumor that those first given out would contain lottery tickets and ruble notes. This, it will be remembered, resulted in one of the most appalling disasters ever known.

Guillotin did not invent the Guillotine. — The decapitating machine employed in France was named after Dr. J. I. Guillotin, who has the reputation of being its inventor; but a somewhat similar machine was used long before he had seen one.

The rude instrument used in Halifax between 1541 and 1650 (*vide* " Tales of a Grandfather ") was the " maiden." A similar decapitating machine was in France called " *la demoiselle;* " in Italy it was known as the "*mannaia.*" But unlike the guillotine they were without any contrivances for binding their victims, and they *chopped* off heads, while the French invention has a sharp sliding knife that slices. All that Dr. Guillotin himself did was, in 1759, publicly to encourage a preference for this means of death as being painless.

Dr. Guillotin on Jan. 21, 1790 (three years to a day before the execution of Louis XVI.), proposed that all executions should take place by decapitation and by a simple mechanism. The motion was referred to a committee of seven, and became a law in October, 1791. C. H. Sanson and Dr. Guillotin tried to devise a machine that should meet all requirements. They examined various German engravings of instruments; also Achille Bocchi's engraving of the mannaia, used as early as the thirteenth century, and the Scotch maiden, which is similar to an instrument used in Persia, and one used in 1632 in Toulouse. A German harpsichord-maker named Schmidt happened to come to Sanson's to play duets with him, and heard Sanson mention the matter. He exclaimed in broken French: "Wait, I think I have what you want!" and with a pencil made a drawing. It was the guillotine with a crescent knife raised between the posts and released by a cord. Louis XVI. suggested substituting a straight-edge set slantingly, forming an acute angle. Experiments were made on three dead bodies, and a man named Guidon erected the first guillotine at a cost of 5,500 francs, and on April 25, 1792, a highwayman named Pelle-

tier was executed by it.   It was at first called
louison or louisette; but the name guillotine won
the day.

Guillotin was not its first victim.   He *nearly*
became a victim of the Revolution, but escaped,
and after the close of his political career resumed
his duties as a physician, became one of the founders of the Academy of Medicine in Paris, and
died May 26, 1814, aged seventy-six.

A New Brougham sweeps Clean. — Lord
Brougham did not invent the carriage that bears
his name.   It was used in Paris long before his
day, but in 1837 he brought one to England from
France and had a coach-maker build one like it,
only lighter, stronger, and more elegant.   It became
popular and was called a *brougham.*

**Jefferson more Democratic than is gen-
erally supposed.** — It is generally stated in
sketches of Thomas Jefferson's life that he showed
his democratic spirit by tying his horse in front of
the Capitol and by simply walking in to be inaugurated.   Contemporary newspaper accounts
state that he was at that time boarding near the
Capitol, and that he walked over to take his part
in the ceremony

CHAPTER XII.

BLUNDERS MADE BY FAMOUS AUTHORS AND OTHERS.

Some of Shakespeare's Slips.

" Then our ship has touched the deserts of Bohemia,"

says Shakespeare in " The Winter's Tale." The ship bearing the infant Perdita is thus pictured as being driven on the coasts of Bohemia, but Bohemia has no seaboard at all.

The couplet,

> " Peace, count the clock—
> The clock has stricken three,"

is found in the dialogue between Brutus and Cassius in Shakespeare's " Julius Cæsar." Yet clocks were not known to the Romans, though sun-dials were; and striking clocks were not invented till some hundreds of years after Cæsar's death.

Bacon, in his essay on " Vain Glory," says : " It was prettily devised of Æsop, the fly sat up on the axletree of the chariot-wheel and said, ' What a dust do I raise.'" A writer in " Notes and Queries " points out that the fable is by Laurentius Abstemius.

London's Highest Ground. — A curious sign, the Boy and Pannier, in Panyer Alley, Newgate street, reads:

> " When you have sought the city round,
>   Yet still this is the highest ground."

But the old rhyme is not true. The highest ground in the city is in Cannon street, where it reaches sixty feet, and not in Newgate Street, where it is only fifty-eight feet.

The Real Story of Robinson Crusoe. — Readers have formed an idea that because Robinson Crusoe became an unwilling dweller on his island through shipwreck, therefore Selkirk, the Scottish sailor on whose marvellous adventures Defoe founded his fascinating story, must have landed there through like circumstances. The exact contrary is true. Selkirk had been roving about the Southern seas as sailing-master of one of the ships that set out on a privateering expedition under the famous navigator Dampier, and being dissatisfied with his ship desired to be put ashore. A few others joined him, and they remained on the island of Juan Fernandez for several months until their vessel returned for them. But Selkirk's lifelong aversion to discipline again manifested itself, and the next time his ship touched at Juan Fernandez he was put ashore *by his own request*, in 1704. All things that could be spared to make him comfortable were freely given — food, tools, clothes, weapons, and ammunition.

After the expiration of four years four months, he was taken off by another privateer, the "Duke and Duchess." His sea-chest, cup, gun, etc. (which Crusoe saved from the wreck), created some sensation when they were exhibited in London on his return, in October, 1711. They are now in the Society of Antiquaries' Museum, Edinburgh. Robinson Crusoe, on the other hand, must have landed on some island east of Panama, and there is good reason to believe that it was the Island of Tobago. But Defoe blunders in locating Juan Fernandez Island on the eastern side of South America.

Defoe makes Another Mistake. — Defoe, in his "History of the Plague," says he was an eye-witness of the experiences he relates. Seeing that the Great Plague of London did not break out till 1665, and that he was born in 1661, this cannot be true. Of course Defoe wrote it as a fiction.

The Story of Baron Münchausen. — The German soldier, Baron Münchausen, was not the author of the book of travels named after him. The absurdly exaggerated fictions in this book were written by an expatriated countryman of his named R. E. Raspe, who published them in England in 1785. Raspe made the Baron the putative author, having become acquainted with the false stories which this officer related, and for which he became notorious after returning from his adventurous campaigns in the Russian service.

The Wrong Bones. —Sir Walter Scott, in the " Fortunes of Nigel," causes David Ramsay to swear " by the bones of the immortal Napier." Napier's bones or " rod " were an apparatus for calculating with ; the invention was attributed to John Napier (1550–1617), but in reality known much earlier. They are still said to be made. It is possible that Ramsay's oath was Sir Walter's wit.

A Mistake in " Ivanhoe." — It is said that the Anglo-" Saxon " called the flesh of the brute he had only to tend " cow," and that his Norman master called it, when prepared for his festive board, " beef." The insinuation here is obvious ; but it is met by the fact that the Norman nobles called the same flesh when alive " beef," but that " the Saxon slave " — as he is called in Scott's " Ivanhoe," and from whence started the erroneous idea that all flesh was carried to the castle-hall — always called it, even when roasted, " cow." " Swine is called pork when carried to the castle-hall to feast among the nobles." But so it was by the nobles when alive. Many infer from this that the swineherd rarely tasted pig, whereas it was his principal food.

Scott makes Another Mistake. — What purports to be the true scene of the murder of Amy is one of the chief points of interest at Kenilworth Castle : the ruins of Mervyn's Tower. Here Amy was lured to death by Varney, at the instigation of the earl. But in connecting the unfortunate Amy with that splendid ruin, Sir Walter Scott has given it an importance which is mere fiction. It is even very doubtful whether Amy ever saw the place; at any rate, Kenilworth was not given to Leicester until three years after her death (1560).

A Gladstonian Error. — Gladstone, in "Gleanings of Past Years," Vol. 1, p. 26, causes Daniel to walk unscathed through the furnace seven times heated.

A Browning Mistake. — Dr. Berdoe, in his Browning Cyclopædia, states that in Prince Hohenstiel-Schwangau we have the description of an imaginary meeting of the exiled Emperor Napoleon III. with a woman of the town. The poem really relates a supposed dream of the emperor at the Tuileries in 1868.

Mistakes about Dick Turpin. — The thief Dick Turpin never rode to York on "Black Bess," and did none of the things popularly associated with his name. In their original form the imaginary exploits of this criminal were written, it has been said, by William Maginn, who must have put them on paper about seventy-five years after the events. But whether this be so or not, Ainsworth's account of them in "Rookwood" was written nearly one hundred years after the criminal's execution (1739), and must necessarily be pure fiction, the newspapers of the day being silent on all points but Turpin's contemptible meanness. Even in ascertainable facts Ainsworth is wrong. Turpin was not born at Thackstead, but at Hampstead; the King who was shot was not "Tom," but Matthew, and the affair took place not at Kilburn, but in Whitechapel.

Cromwell had no Illegitimate Children. — The Abbé Prévost, author of "Manon Lescaut," while he was in London wrote a book which purported to be the "Story of Mr. Cleveland, natural son of Cromwell or the English philosopher." Part of it was published in 1732, and the whole work in eight volumes in 1739. An English translation came out in 1734–5. There was no historical authority for the birth of any natural children to Cromwell.

Milton in Error.

> "Till the dappled dawn doth rise,
> And at my window bid good-morrow
> Through the twisted eglantine."

Thus ends the forty-first line of Milton's "L'Allegro." The eglantine does not "twist," but Milton was mistaken in giving this name to the honeysuckle. The eglantine is the prickly sweet-briar of our gardens.

Pope misled Warburton. — Pope, in a note on "Measure for Measure," states that the story was taken from Cintheo's novel, Dec. 8, Nov. 5, meaning decade 8, novela 5. Warburton in his edition of Shakespeare filled out the contractions as December 8, November 5.

There Never was a Hannah Glasse. — Any one who has read Sala's "Journal" will not soon forget that there is such a book as Mrs. Glasse's "Art of

Cookery made Plain and Easy" (1746). But not all may know that "Hannah Glasse" is as much a myth as was Sairey Gamp's [1] Mrs. Harris. The real compiler, as Dilly, the publisher, told Johnson, was Dr. John Hill. The choice of a woman's name arose through business prudence on the publisher's part. Nevertheless, the alleged Hannah has been often treated as a real individual, as, for instance, in an American publication wherein it is stated: "Mrs. Glasse wrote other books on similar subjects."

The mention of Dr. Johnson calls to mind his erstwhile pupil, David Garrick, and those who know anything of the great actor perhaps remember that it is Hill that figures in David's stinging epigram: "His farces are physic — his physic a farce is!" Another association is the ironical proverb: "First catch your hare," which, though sometimes attributed to "Mrs. Glasse," is not found in "The Art of Cookery," but in all likelihood was suggested by the words, "Take your hare when it is cased," *i.e.*, skinned.

A Star that is not a Star. —

> "Till clombe [2] above the eastern bar
> The horned moon, with one bright star
> Within the nether tip."

---

[1] In Dickens' "Martin Chuzzlewit," a fat old woman "with a husky voice and a moist eye," engaged in the profession of nursing. She is always quoting her mythical friend Mrs. Harris, and her affection for the bottle is proverbial. From a part of her varied belongings a very stumpy umbrella is called a gamp.

[2] Climbed.

The "star" mentioned in this quotation, from the third part of Coleridge's "Ancient Mariner," is not a star, but a lofty lunar peak from which the light of the sun is reflected, and which may be seen sometimes on clear evenings, when the moon is in the first quarter, in the shadowed disc at some distance from the bright crescent.

Byron's Blunder. — The last line of Byron's "Marino Faliero" reads:

"The gory head rolls down the Giant's Steps."

The steps alluded to are in the courtyard of the Ducal Palace, Venice, and are known as the Giant's Staircase, because of the colossal statues of Mars and Neptune on its summit; and by the "gory head" is meant that of Marino Faliero, one of the doges of Venice. Unfortunately this sovereign was decapitated before this stairway had been built; but it is a fact that he was beheaded in the palace.

A Mistaken Prophecy. — In view of the recent "recrudescence" of interest in Lord Byron and his works, George Borrow's cynical description of Byron's funeral, in Chapter XXXIX. of "Lavengro," is rather amusing. He says: "A time will come when he will be out of fashion and forgotten." Then, as if afraid to venture such a prediction, he adds: "And yet I don't know; didn't he write 'Childe Harold' and that ode? Yes, he wrote 'Childe Harold' and that ode. Then a time will scarcely come when he will be forgotten. Lords, squires, and cockneys may pass away, but a time will scarcely come when ' Childe Harold' and that ode will be forgotten."

The Wrong Sumner. — The Rev. H. R. Haweis, in his book "My Hundred Thousand Miles of Travel," states that he met Charles Sumner in 1893 at San Francisco, after his sermon at the Golden Gate Hall ; that Sumner went to Washington in 1895, and " defeated a pretty little Southern Pacific job ; " that he was in England in 1883, and tried in vain to get into St. James' Church, owing to the crush. Charles Sumner died on March 17, 1874. Mr. Haweis afterwards tried to convince the world that he referred to *Senator* Charles A. Sumner of the Pacific slope. This Charles Sumner was never a senator.

Victor Hugo's Mathematical Blunder. — Victor Hugo lays the scene of one of his novels in England, but makes the drollest blunders in regard to English life and customs. • Like almost all Frenchmen, he misspells English proper names. For instance, he transforms the Firth of Forth into the First of the Fourth !

Dumas creates an English Village. — Alexandre Dumas, in "Twenty Years After," brings the fallen King Charles to a village named Ryston, which is not to be found in the kingdom ; moreover he assigned to it a locality so near London that, even if it did exist, the journey from Derby thither could not possibly have been performed in one day, at the period and under the circumstances referred to in the narrative.   His whole account of the execution as well as of the blowing up of the felucca is an extravagant fiction which makes an element of undesigned comedy in a tragedy.

Carlyle's Queer English. — At a sale that took place in London in June, 1896, a pane of glass said to have been inscribed by Carlyle brought £11 5s. The lines, quoted in the "Athenæum," read :

> " Little did my mother think,
> That night she cradled me,
> What land I was to travel to,
> Or what death I should die.
> Oh, foolish thee ! "

The last line only was by Carlyle.   But the whole poem was wrongly copied.   It reads :

> " Little did my mother think,
> The day she cradled me,
> What land I was to travel in,
> Or what death I should die.
> Oh, foolish me ! "

The first four lines are from a well-known ballad.

Errors of Translation. — The similarity between many English and foreign words, even where the meanings are different, often mislead translators into odd mistakes.   A translator of a Spanish book caused a man wrestling with another to " smell his opponent's powerful breath," instead of " perceiving his labored breathing." The German translator of Anna Karénina, misled by the Slavonic epigraph of the story, translates it to mean " Vengeance is sweet, I play the ace," instead of " Vengeance is mine, I will repay." The Slavonic for I is **Az**, while the Russian is **Ya**.

African She-goats. — In a book on " The Illustrious Henris," published in 1858, the editor translates the Latin words *Affra capella* as follows :

" A she-goat's skin receives his father's bones." Mr. T. E. Bridget points out that Floto, in his history of Henry IV., states that the emperor's body lay in a stone sarcophagus in the unconsecrated chapel of St. Afra at Spiers. So that *Affra capella*, the words the Rev. F. C. Hingeston mistook for African she-goat, really mean the Chapel of St. Afra.

Harmless as Doves. — In the New Testament passage, " Be ye therefore wise as serpents and *harmless* as doves," the Greek word is incorrectly translated, though the right meaning is indicated in the margin as simple. It means unmixed, therefore guileless ; and not hornless, and therefore without means of doing harm. Another odd misconception is found in the authorized version of the Book of Baruch, where it says : " Prepare ye manna and offer upon the altar of the Lord our God." The word manna there stands for *mincha*, an offering.

Goggle-eyed Saints. — Wyclif mistook the Keltic expression goggle-eyed, which means with full, rolling eyes, for the Latin *cocles* (compare the Greek *Kuklops*, one-eyed), and translated Mark IX., 47: " It is good to thee for to entre gogil-yzed into rewme of God, than havynge twey yzen for to be sent into helle of fier."

Good Yeeres that are Bad. — Shakespeare mistook the name of the gougères, a filthy disease, and called it the *good yeeres*. "The good yeeres shall devour them flesh and fell." But in this he had fellowship in many other writers of his century and later.

A Glove for a Shoe. — In the English rendering of Ruth IV., 7, 8, it reads: "A man plucked off his shoe and gave it to his neighbor; and this was a testimony in Israel. Therefore the kinsman said unto Boaz, ' Buy it for thee.' So he drew off his shoe." The Hebrew *nagal* is said to mean sandal only when it is followed by *regil*, the foot; but when it stands by itself it means glove. In one of the German versions it is correctly translated *hand-schuh*, or glove.

Tulips and Turbans. — Spenser, in his " Faërie Queene," speaks of " old Cybele " as

> " Wearing a Diademe embattild wide
> With hundred turrets like a turribant."

But the word has nothing to do with turrets or tops, nor has it anything to do with the Latin *torquere*, to twist. It is said to come from the Persian *du*, two, and *lai*, a fold. The word tulip has the same origin: one of its former names was Dalmatian or Turk's Cap.

The Street of the Golden Dragon. — The Street of the Golden Dragon in Hong Kong is said by Andrew Wilson to have derived its name from the call of the Chinese girls, who, sitting at the windows, would greet the sailors visiting them with the cry " Come 'long, Jack." Hence it came to be known as " Come 'Long" Street, which the Chinese glorified into Kum Lung, meaning Golden Dragon.

Deceptions about Dickens. — The "Old Curiosity Shop," in Portsmouth Street, Lincoln's Inn Fields, was not " immortalized by Charles Dickens." The novelist's son calls the building " a complete fraud." At Broadstairs, in Kent, the title of " Bleak House" has been applied to a building once known as Fort House on the cliff above the harbor, and hence many, especially in those parts, believe that " Bleak House" was written there. Much of Dickens' work was done there. " Bleak House" was written elsewhere.

The Mouse Tower. — Southey's poem of the Mouse tower on the Rhine is founded on a misconception. It was originally the mautthurm or tollhouse, which became corrupted into Mäuseturm, and the legend was manufactured to suit.

Peeled, but not Skinned. — In the eighteenth chapter of Isaiah, messengers are said to be sent out to a nation scattered and peeled. A marginal reading gives " outspread and polished." But the

word peeled does not signify stripped of skin or
pell, but bald, — "pylled as one that wanteth heare,"
— and hence robbed, as in the word pillage.

Grolier not a Binder. — It is a mistake to
suppose that Grolier, for whom the well-known
club is named, was a bookbinder; he was a book
collector.

Where Shelley was drowned. —

"Drowned by the upsetting of his boat in the Gulf of
Spezia."

So reads the epitaph on Shelley's monument
erected at Christchurch, Hants, by his son, Sir
Percy, and Lady Shelley; and dictionaries and
encyclopædias also perpetuate the error. The
boat really foundered in the roads of Viaregio.
The seaport of Viaregio is only fourteen miles
northwest of Pisa, while the Gulf of Spezia,
following the coast-line, is not far short of fifty
miles.

Queen Bess's Pocket-pistol. —

"Load me well and keep me clean,
And I'll carry a ball to Calais Green,"

is popularly supposed to be a translation of the
Flemish inscription on the cannon given Queen
Elizabeth by the Low Countries in recognition of
her efforts to protect them and their religion at
Dover. The "pocket pistol" is now removed to a
less conspicuous part of the castle.

The common idea is that the gun is able to sweep the French port which lies in front of it. The Calais in question could not refer to the French town, but to a place called Calais Green, about one and a half miles from Dover; but according to the "Daily Telegraph" of May 26, 1894, the refrain is, however, "completely erroneous," as the words really mean:

> "Over hill and dale I can throw a ball;
> My name is Breaker of Mound and Wall."

An Untrustworthy Gravestone. —

Tho: **Parr** of ye county of Sallop Borne in A^o: 1483. He lived in ye reignes of Ten Princes viz: K. Edw. 4 K. Ed. 5 K. Rich. 3 K. Hen. 7 K. Hen. 8 K. Edw. 6 Q. Ma. Eliz. K. Ja. and K. Charles Aged 152 years and was Buried Here Novemb 15 1635.

The inscription is over the grave of Old Parr in the south transept of Westminster "Abbey;" but though the gravestone is in such a place, nevertheless it is absolutely untrustworthy.

Parr's pretensions, like those of another veteran impostor, Henry Jenkins, aged 169, were ruthlessly exposed by the late Mr. W. T. Thoms (the original editor of "Notes and Queries"). Parr was an exceptionally old man, yet certainly he lived not more than a year or two over a century.

The fabulists say his son lived to the age of 113, his grandson to 109, his great-grandson to 124, his great-granddaughter, who died in Skiddy's Alms-house, Cork, October, 1792, to 103.   To these may be added another grandson, John Newell, Esq , of Michaelstown, Ireland, who died at the age of 102. But the fact is that he left *no* children; for his son lived but ten weeks and his daughter only three weeks!

The King's Library. — Above the south door in the stately gallery in the British Museum known as the King's Library there is an inscription which runs as follows:

This library, collected by George the Third, was given by His Most Gracious Majesty George the Fourth, in the third year of his reign, A.D. MDCCCXXIII.

This statement is misleading.   When George the Fourth was hard pressed for money he desired to sell his father's collection, and at one time the books were in danger of getting into the hands of a royal purchaser abroad.   The king was approached on the subject, and a bargain was struck that he should be secretly paid for the library, but that it should be given out that he had presented it to the nation. For his alleged generosity his Majesty was actually thanked by the House of Commons in terms of the "strongest gratitude."

The "Daily Chronicle," March 21, 1895, says: "A tradition of the British Museum asserts that a portion of the library was actually placed on board a ship to be sent to Russia.   In the centre of the

king's library is displayed the letter of gift of the
collection from George the Fourth to Lord Liverpool.   Such is certainly worth keeping as a curiosity ; still, an official statement as to the true facts of
the case ought to be appended."

The Iron Duke. — This sobriquet for the Duke
of Wellington came from an iron steamship plying
between Liverpool and Dublin ; its owners called it
the *Duke of Wellington*, but the public, as they will,
nicknamed it the "Iron Duke."   The humorous
association was a transference obviously inevitable.

Mercator should be Kremer. — Mercator is
properly Gerhard Kremer, a Belgian geographer,
born in 1512.   And the system of map-drawing
called Mercator's   should   therefore   be   called
Kremer's projection.   But, according to the pe-
dantic custom of the time, his name, meaning a
merchant, was Latinized into "Mercator."   Gill's
"Student's Geography" says the inventor's real
name was Kauffman, but this is wrong.

CHAPTER XIII.

MISQUOTATIONS AND OTHER LITERARY STUMBLING-BLOCKS.

Do not quote, but if You do, quote Correctly. — Any one depending on the memory for quotations is almost certain to make verbal alterations, and sometimes will quite change the sense-There are few things more vexatious than to hear hackneyed quotations introduced into common speech, unless it is to hear them misquoted.

As generally quoted, the line from "Richard III," Act I., Scene i., beginning "Now is the winter of our discontent," is made to mean : "At this present time we are suffering." But the following line, "Made glorious summer by this sun of York," shows that the "now" modifies the verb "made," and this, of course, gives the words a diametrically opposite meaning.

So with the line from "Troilus and Cressida," Act III., Scene iii., "One touch of nature makes the whole world kin; " for whenever quoted it invariably deviates from the original meaning. The "touch of nature " is now used to mean a touch of joy, or the wound of sorrow, or, indeed, any susceptibility that opens a source of sympathy to all

men.   But all this was far from the mind of
Shakespeare.   What he intended to depict was
foolish humanity united in praising everything
that happened to be merely new fashioned, as the
context will show:

> " One touch of nature makes the whole world kin,
> That all, with one consent, praise new-born gawds,
> Though they are made and moulded of things past."

Equally interesting are these lines from the
" Tempest," and found on Shakespeare's monument in Westminster " Abbey ":

> " The cloud-capp'd towers, the gorgeous palaces,
> The solemn temple, the great globe itself,
> Yea, all which it inhabit, shall dissolve;
> And like the baseless fabric of this vision
> Leave not a wreck behind."

But by referring to Act IV., Scene i., it will be
seen that the penultimate line is a transposition,
and that another has been omitted.   In Clark and
Wright's text the lines run thus:

> " *And like the baseless fabric of this vision,*
> The cloud-capped towers, the gorgeous palaces,
> The solemn temples, the great globe itself,
> Yea, all which it inhabit, shall dissolve,
> *And, like this insubstantial pageant faded,*
> Leave not a rack behind."

It is noticeable that " wreck " in one line becomes " rack " in the corresponding line.   Imagine

the absurdity of a "vision" leaving behind it
"*a wreck.*" What Shakespeare actualiy wrote
was " rack," and what he meant, as in other pas-
sages as well, was in the sense of drifting vapor;
cf. " Hamlet," II., ii., 506 ; " Antony," IV., xiv., 10,
etc. Thus Shakespeare is not properly quoted
even on his monument.

Another Misquoted Epitaph. — Wren's familiar epitaph is frequently misprinted " *Si monumen-
tum quæris circumspice.*" The word which the
great architect's son wrote in the inscription over
the north transept door of St. Paul's Cathedral was
not " *quæris,*" but " *requires.*" The usually reli-
able " Murray's Handbook to London " inserts the
word " *quæris* " in the inscription.

Coleridge Misrepresented. — Very few, if put
to the test, could complete correctly Coleridge's
line : " Water, water, everywhere." The almost
universal rendering is : " And not a drop to drink."
The " Echo " of March 19, 1895, prints it thus, and
in quotation marks too! What Coleridge wrote in
"The Ancient Mariner" was : " Nor any drop to
drink."

Others of the Same Sort. — Another well-
known quotation from " The Fire Worshippers "
suffers in the first line : " 'Twas ever thus from
childhood's hour " is the usual reading. What
Thomas Moore actually says is : " Oh, ever thus."
Misquoters also nonsensically interject " happy "
between " childhood's " and " hour ; " the comple-

mentary line being: "I've seen my fondest hopes decay."

Tennyson's "Irresponsible indolent reviewers" is frequently misquoted as "Irresponsible ignorant reviewers."

"Fresh fields and pastures new" should be, according to Milton's "Lycidas," line 193, "Fresh woods and pastures new;" and to correct the erratum, "The human form divine," we must go to his "Paradise Lost," Book III., and read:

> " . . . Thus with the year
> Seasons return; but not to me returns
> Day, or the sweet approach of even or morn,
> Or sight of vernal bloom, or summer's rose,
> Or flocks, or herds, or human face divine."

"Spare the rod and spoil the child" is not from the Bible. It may be as quoted in "Hudibras," Part II., Canto i., verse 45, either a misquotation or a quotation attributed to the wrong source. Certainly Solomon did not say it. What he said was: "He that spareth the rod hateth his son."

And the word "rod" in this connection does not stand necessarily for a leather strap or a willow stick, but as a symbol of guidance and correction. Compare: "His rod and His staff they comfort me."

In Gray's "Elegy" will be found the correction of "The even tenor of their way;" Gray wrote "The noiseless tenor of their way."

"The end justifies the means" is a free transla-

tion of " *Cui licitus est finis, etiam licent media.*"
" Where the end is lawful, the means thereto are
lawful also "— the maxim of the Jesuit writer,
Busenbaum. The reference is his "Medulla Theo-
logiæ Moralis," and the precise place 6. 6. 2.

Further Instances. — " When Greek meets
Greek, then comes the tug of war," should be, if correctly quoted, " When Greeks joined Greeks, then
was the tug of war" (see Nathaniel's " Alexander
the Great," Act X., Scene ii.), or if one wishes to
make the present tense applicable to it, then use
"joins," not " meets."

" Every mickle makes a muckle " is a misrender-
ing of a familiar Scotch saying, and is absurd.
" Mickle " and " muckle " are different spellings of
one and the same word, but " mickle " is generally
understood to mean " little; " even then the inter-
pretation is hardly warranted, for it is obvious that
every " little " will not make a " much," though
many " littles " may. The true rendering runs:
" Mony a little maks a meikle," meaning in
English, " Many smalls make a big."

A vulgar (and sometimes intentional) error of
misquoting the conclusion of our " duty toward our
neighbor " makes it run, " to do my duty in that
state of life unto which it *has pleased* God to call
me," whereas the Catechism says, " unto which it
shall please God to call me." Dickens makes the
same error in " Bleak House " (see Chaps. III. and
XXVIII.).

" You have hit the nail on the head " (" Rabelais,"
Book III., Chap. XXXIV.).   Unthinking people
almost always say the " right nail," which is absurd.
The much more correct meaning is: " He who is
quick to use his advantages hits the nail on the
head, while others hammer round it," and observation will prove that the reference to the " right
nail " means this in nine instances to one where it
is a contradistinction to the finger-nail.

> " The Knights are dust,
> And their good swords are rust;
> Their souls are with the saints, we trust."

This is a misquotation found in " Ivanhoe,"
Chap. VIII., and elsewhere often repeated. The
correct lines are:

> " The Knight's bones are dust,
> And his good sword rust;
> His soul is with the saints, I trust."
>
> (Coleridge, " The Knight's Tomb.")

" He that runs may read " should be " he may
run that readeth it."

**Quotations like Iron-filings cluster around
Some Famous Men.** — Allied with misquotations
are sententious sayings wrongly attributed to
famous persons. Like iron-filings around a magnet, witty remarks are apt to attach themselves to
some person with a reputation for cleverness.
Thus many brilliant *jeux d'esprit* are fathered on

Richard Brinsley Sheridan, who took them from D'Argenson and others. Abraham Lincoln is made to originate a great number of witty stories. Thomas G. Appleton did not invent the name for Nahant, "Cold Roast Boston;" nor did he wish that some one would expose a shorn lamb on the corner of Park Street, that the Lord might temper the wind to it.

Talleyrand and Fouché. — Talleyrand did not invent the expression, "It is the beginning of the end": it may be found in Shakespeare's "Midsummer Night's Dream" (Act. V., Scene i.). Neither did he say of the Bourbons, "*Ils n'ont rien appris ni rien oublié*," "They have learned nothing and forgotten nothing." It is found in a letter written in January, 1796, by the Chevalier de Panat to Mallet du Pan. Nor again did he invent the phrase "Words were given man to disguise his thoughts" ("*La parole a été donnée à l'homme pour déguiser sa pensée*"). Voltaire uses it in his fourteenth dialogue, and it is quoted by Oliver Goldsmith in "The Bee." It really goes back to a hoary antiquity.

"It is worse than a crime: it is a blunder." Talleyrand was not the author of these words, neither is it a correct quotation. In their original form the words were by Joseph Fouché [1] (1763–1820), Minister of Police under Napoleon. "It is worse than a crime: it is political fault, words which I record because they have been repeated and attributed to others."

---

[1] "Memoirs of Fouché."

The aphorism *Le style c'est l'homme* would apply still more forcibly if it were restored to the form which Buffon gave it: *Le style c'est l'homme même* — is the *very* man.

Words that Some Great Men never spoke. — Dr. Johnson is said to have said, " Let us take a walk down Fleet Street " (" Old and New London," Vol. I., p. 34). G. A. Sala, in his " Life and Adventures," says: " To this periodical I gave the name of ' Temple Bar,' and from a rough sketch of mine of the old Bar, which blocked the way in Fleet Street, Mr. Percy Macquoid drew an admirable frontispiece. As a motto I *imagined* a quotation from Boswell: ' " And now, sir," said Dr. Johnson, " we will take a walk down Fleet Street." ' To the best of my knowledge and belief, Dr. J. never said a word about taking a walk down Fleet Street ; but my innocent *supercherie* was, I fancy, implicitly believed in for at least a generation by the majority of magazine readers."

The doctor's exact words, " Let us take a walk down Cheapside," are found in George Lewes' " History of Philosophy." They, or the somewhat similar ones of Boswell, must have been running through Sala's mind at the time.

An Epitaph Falsely Attributed. — The well-known epitaph :

> " Sidney's sister, Pembroke's mother,
> Death, ere thou hast slain another
> Learn'd and fair and good as she,
> Time shall throw a dart at thee,"

on the sister of Sir Philip Sidney, author of "Arcadia," is usually ascribed to Ben Jonson and placed in the editions of his works; but it is found in a manuscript collection of William Browne's poems in the British Museum (Lansdowne MS., No. 777), and Sir Egerton Brydges ascribes the authorship to him in his edition of Browne's poems.

In Westminster "Abbey" "Rare Ben Jonson's" patronymic is misspelled with an "h" in three different inscriptions.

Cambronne at Waterloo. — The story is often repeated that at the battle of Waterloo (June 18, 1815) Hugh Baron Halkett (pronounced Hacket) demanded that General Cambronne should surrender and that Cambronne replied: "*La garde meurt et* [*mais*] *ne se rend pas.*" Cambronne all his life long, in public and in private, denied having said the words attributed to him, and an eye-witness declares that his words as his horse was shot under him were: "*Je me rends,*" "I surrender." The words were invented by a Paris journalist, Rougemont, two days after the battle, in the "Indépendant," and are engraved on a monument to Cambronne at Nantes. Other French writers, Victor Hugo, for instance, in "Les Misérables," declare that Cambronne's only exclamation was the untranslatable word, "*Merde!*"

The famous words: "Up, Guards, and at them!" were never uttered by the Duke of Wellington at Waterloo: and, moreover, it was not the Guards, but the 52d Light Infantry, who broke the advancing column of the French Imperial Guards in the final charge.

And here must be thrown overboard another cherished tradition. Who does not know Byron's lines — " Within a window'd niche in that high hall sat Brunswick's fated chieftain " —referring to the revelry in the ballroom of the Duchess of Richmond at Brussels the night before Waterloo, which was suddenly interrupted by " the cannons' opening roar"? The " high hall" has been recently the subject of a most animated discussion, and has been found to be, alas! nothing more than a coachmaker's low-roofed show-room hired by the duchess for the occasion. It still may be seen in the Rue de la Blanchisserie by the inquisitive tourist.

Galileo did not say E pur si Muove. — The story that Galileo, when compelled by the Inquisition to recant and confess, in June, 1633, muttered, " And yet it does move," and that he had his eyes put out in consequence, is a late fiction. He remained in confinement only three days, and when released lived in the villa Medici, occupied by the Tuscan ambassador. He afterwards returned on foot to Sienna.

Louis XIV. and the State. — There is no historic foundation for the story that Louis XIV., a boy under sixteen, strode into Parliament in April, 1695, and flourishing his riding-whip exclaimed to the president of Parliament: " *L'état! c'est moi, monsieur!* "

Kosciusko and the End of Poland. — It is frequently stated in histories that Kosciusko, at the battle of Maciejowice, Oct. 10, 1794, as he fell from his horse, exclaimed, " *Finis Poloniæ*," " The end of Poland."

> " And Freedom shrieked as Kosciusko fell."

In a letter that he wrote Oct. 31, 1803, he distinctly repudiates having made any such derogatory remark. " It would be a crime in the mouth of any Pole, much more in mine."

Remarks attributed to Wrong Person. — Napoleon did not say, " Austria is always behind with an idea, with an army," but William Pitt said : " The gentlemen of Vienna are always behindhand with an idea, a year, and an army." Neither did Napoleon say, " Scratch the Russian and you will find the Tartar " (" *Grattez le Russe, vous trouverez le Cosaque* ") ; it was said by Prince Karl Josef de Ligne ; nor the phrase, " He is fond of washing his soiled linen in public ; " it is Voltaire's.

Huss did not say " Sancta Simplicitas " or pun on his Own Name. — The story goes that when Huss was bound to the stake an old woman came bringing a bundle of faggots and threw it on the pile which was to consume him, and that Huss exclaimed, " *O Sancta Simplicitas !* " (" Oh, holy simplicity ! "), and that immediately after he uttered this prophecy, which contains a punning reference to the meaning of his Slavonic name, Huss (*gus*, a goose) : " This day ye burn a goose, but in a hundred years a white swan will come, which ye will not be able to burn. " [1]

It is a pure fabrication. Neither is it certain that Luther said : " Here I stand ; I have no other alternative ; God help me ! Amen." [2]

Only the last four words are historic.

All is lost save Honor. — Francois I. in announcing to his mother the capture of Pavia, Feb. 24, 1525, did not write, " *Tout est perdu fors l'honneur.*" His autograph letter still exists. He wrote : " Madame, that I make you acquainted with the whole extent of my misfortune I will say, that of all that I had nothing remains to me except honor and life." (" *De toutes choses ne m'est demeuré que l'honneur, et la vie qui est saulve.*")

The Crime of Youth. — The elder Pitt did not use the expression " The atrocious crime of being a young man," in his reply to Walpole on being taunted on account of his youth. The words were composed and reported in the " Gentleman's Magazine " by Dr. Johnson, who was not present, but who, from an abstract communicated to him, colored Pitt's speech " with his own peculiar style and dic-

---

[1] " Heut braten sie eine Gans,
    Das bin ich, armen Hans !
    Nach hundert Jahren kommt ein Schwan,
    Den werden sie ungebraten l'an."

[2] " Hier stehe ich; ich kann nicht anders; Gott helfe mir ! Amen."

tion." Johnson is reported as saying, "That speech I wrote in a garret in Exeter street."

Shakespeare vs. Barnfield. — "The Passionate Pilgrim" can of course be found in any volume of Shakespeare, but the latter part, beginning with :

> "As it fell upon a day
>   In the merry month of May,
>   Sitting in a pleasant shade,
>   Which a grove of myrtle made,"

was not composed by him, but by Richard Barnfield, who called it an "Address to the Nightingale." Ellis says in his "Specimens," Vol. II.: "This song, often attributed to Shakespeare, is now confidently assigned to Barnfield; it is found in his book of ' Poems in Divers Humours,' published in 1598."

Other Proverbs. — "Blude is thicker than water." Because this proverb is found in " Guy Mannering," Chap. XXXVIII., it is nearly always ascribed to Scott, but it was very common in the seventeenth century. It is found as early as 1670 in John Ray's and other collections of proverbs.

" Evil communications corrupt good manners" was not composed by St. Paul, but by Menander, the Grecian comic poet, and most likely the apostle was only using an already familiar proverb.

" God tempers the wind to the shorn lamb" has a sufficiently biblical ring about it to account for the common impression that it appears in a passage of the Old Testament. The original source is not known. It occurs in Sterne's "Sentimental Journey," but it is much older than that, for in a collection of proverbs published as far back as 1594 we find " *Dieu mésure le froid à la brebis tondue* " (" God proportions the cold to the shorn lamb ").

A person wishing to convey a message of condolence to a woman who had lost her husband, wrote it: " God tempers the wind to the stolen lamb." " In the midst of life we are in death " is also wrongly taken to be from the Bible. It was transferred to the Book of Common Prayer from an old German hymn in Latin — an antiphon said to have been composed by Notker, a monk of St. Gall, in 911, while watching some workmen building a bridge at Martinsbrücke, in peril of their lives. It forms the groundwork of Luther's antiphon, " De Morte." Nor is the well-known line, " The merciful man is merciful to his beast," to be found in the Scriptures, though " A righteous man regardeth the life of his beast " may be (Proverbs XII., 10). On the other hand, comparatively few persons seem aware that the expression " The skin of my teeth " appears in Job XIX., 20.

The every-day quotation " Every man has his price " is evidently a misquotation of Sir Robert Walpole's words: referring to certain factious or profligate adversaries and their adherents resembling themselves, he said, " All *these* men have their price ! " (*Vide* Cox's " Life of Walpole," Vol. I., p. 757.)

A Nation of Shopkeepers. — It is commonly thought that Napoleon the First was the author of the expression " a nation of shopkeepers." Even Wheeler, in his " Names of Fiction," thus attributes it: " A contemptuous appellation bestowed upon the English by Napoleon Bonaparte." But it was used by Adam Smith in his " Wealth of Nations," when Napoleon was only six years old, and at that time every English statesman knew it " by heart." Through translation the phrase naturally caught the fancy of French politicians, and some twenty years later its popularity was permanently assured by Barère, who, in the French Convention of June 11, 1794, publicly bestowed the already familiar catch-phrase upon England. He said, in allusion to Howe's battle of June 1st: " Let Pitt, then, boast of his victory to his nation of shopkeepers."

Sheep and Tar. — The English sometimes speak of " Losing a ship for a ha'p'orth of tar." But who ever heard of a ship the timbers of which required tar to hold them together? Substitute " sheep " for " ship " and the absurdity no longer appears, for clearly the allusion is to the shep-herd's economical practice of marking his flock. It is as well to compare :

> " And judge you now what fooles those are
> Will loose a hog [1] for a ha'p'orth of tar."
>
> (" Maronides " (Geo. Philip's), 1673, Bk. VI., p. 22.)

---

[1] " Hog " is used in Yorkshire and some other counties for a sheep a year old.

" The Dog and his Shadow." — There is a confusion of words veiled under this phrase. It is, of course, obvious that it was not the shadow that the greedy animal saw in the brook, but the reflection of himself with the piece of meat in his mouth.

Mistakes in Given Names. — Fond parents of new-born children are often at a loss for a name to confer on them. Sometimes ludicrous mistakes are made. A father, shortly after the beginning of the present century, was greatly interested in the French Revolution, and wishing to commemorate it in the name of a daughter called her Ça-ira, but not knowing French pronounced it Kayiry. She was always known to the younger generation as Aunt Kayiry. It is a mistake to give a girl the name Evelyn, which is the masculine form of the word; if applied to a girl it should be Evelina, or Eveline, or Avelina.

Cocaine and Alkaloids. — A writer in "Notes and Queries" says that it is particularly exasperating to hear cocaine pronounced as two syllables. He says: " It cannot be too emphatically insisted that this word should be pronounced as a word of three syllables, *co-ca-ine*, signifying as it does the active principle of the narcotic shrub coca, which by the way has nothing to do with cocoa."

Another writer takes exception to the statement that " the termination ine [in] always denotes the alkaloid or active principle of anything." It is true morphine is the active principle of opium; nicotine, of tobacco; quinine, of cinchona; strychnine, of nux vomica; caffeïne, of coffee; but there are iodine, bromine, glycerine, chlorine, crocine, and carmine which do not denote alkaloids, nor is an alkaloid necessarily the active principle of a thing; for instance, " opium yields, beside morphine, papaverine, thebaine, codeine, narcotine, narceine, and probably several more, each of which has properties of its own, none of which has precisely the same value as any other."

Common Mistakes in French. — Some of the most decorous and cleverest-looking intruders in the realm of language have no right to their respectability. Take this one: " A duel *à l'outrance* " (from the " Touchstone of Life," April, 1897). There is not such an expression known in French, yet English writers nearly always use it when they really mean *à outrance* (" to the utmost "— " in the strongest terms "). *Exposé* is another. Too often this is written as French for " exposure," but *exposition* is the right term. Next, *gasconnade* deserves two " n's," although it does not always get them. Then there is the fanciful *nom de plume*. No Frenchman ever uses it. The French term is *nom de guerre*, properly applied to assumed names, such as *Athos*, *Porthos*, and *Aramis*, which French gentlemen often used till they had won their spurs, or as long as they wished to remain unknown. Custom may have sanctioned an error of this kind, but it cannot make an error justifiable. And we have yet to learn, in spite of music-hall programs, that a Frenchman addresses his envelopes with either of the horrible Anglo-French constructions, *Mons.* or *Mdlle.* Again, *gourmet* sometimes takes the place intended for *gourmand;* the meaning is, however, very different, as *gourmet* signifies, in French, a judge of wine, and *gourmand* a glutton, or, more mildly, a gastronomist.

A most egregious blunder is to write *coûte qui coûte* for "cost what it may," for then it has the ridiculous meaning of "cost whom it may." The proper phrase is *coûte que coûte.* A weekly paper says : "This sort of *coute qui coute* policy has operated before." But it is surprising to find the distortion even made by Pope in his "Imitation of Horace," Bk. II., Sat. VI. :

> " . . . loved his friend, and had a soul,
> Knew what was handsome, and would do't,
> On just occasions, *coute qui coute.*"

Double entendre, which some writers seem to think is French, has never existed in France. Perhaps *double entente* is intended, but even then a word cannot *be*, but may *have*, *a double entente*, as *mot à double entente.* It is a mistake to tack an "of" on the French expression *à propos.* It is better not to use the expression.

Common Mistakes in Latin. — "*Dulce domum*" is not, as so often supposed, "sweet home;" and this in spite of the fact that it is sometimes seen as the name of suburban villas. A " sweet home " would be, in correct Latin, *dulcis domus; " dulce domum,"* on the other hand, means " (that) sweet (word), homeward," from the song sung at Winchester College at the close of the term. In utter defiance of grammar, the surplus money offered for distribution by insurance offices is usually called " *bonus*" (a good *man*) instead of " *bonum* " (a good *thing*).

In the English Church Catechism, in answer to the question, " What is your name ? " the answer should not be " N. or M.," but " N. or NN.," *i.e.*, Latin *nomen aut nomina*, name or names. The printers started the mistake.

As a general rule it is a mistake to use foreign words when English words would serve as well. But if foreign words must be used, they should be correctly used.

" **Pitfalls of Pedantry.**"—It is a mistake to put:

Aide-de-camps for aides-de-camp ;

Chef-d'œuvres for chefs-d'œuvre ;

Handsful for handfuls ;

Cherubims for cherubim or cherubs. Cherubims is given in 2 Sam. VI., 2, as the plural of cherub, and in conversation the same error frequently occurs. Of course if the inflection im is used the s is not required. Compare seraph — seraphim ; Baal — Baalim (the images of Baal).

On the other hand, Shakespeare, in "The Tempest," makes Prospero say to Miranda,

"Oh, a cherubim
Thou wast that did preserve me."

Animalculæ for animalcula;
Omnibi for omnibuses;
Phantasmagoria for phantasmagoriæ;
Apparata for apparatus;
Ignorami for ignoramuses;
Hiati for hiatuses;
Phenomenons for phenomena;
Mussulmen for mussulmans.

On the other hand, it is a mistake to speak of:

A dicta for a dictum;
A data for a datum;
An ephemeræ for an ephemera;
A genera for a genus;
A phenomena for a phenomenon;
Chinee for Chinese;
Portuguee for Portuguese.

Mr. Palmer calls such blunders the pitfalls of pedantry. But many similar blunders have been so widely adopted that they have become recognized as correct, thus:

Minnow is a false singular for minnows;
Grouse for grice; because, forsooth, mouse is the singular of mice;
Pea for pease (as if chee for cheese!);

Sherry is an assumed singular of sherris, for Spanish Xeres, wine of Xeres;

Cherry is an assumed singular of cherries, which stands for French *cérise.*

Many words have lost or gained letters by reason of the propinquity of an article:

Apron should properly be napron, from the French naperon, nappe, cloth;

Auger should be nauger, from nav and gor, a wheel-borer;

Adder is really nadder;

Newt is an eft;

Orange should be norange, from Sanskrit naranga, through the Persian and Arabic. The Sanskrit word means bright and is applied to a snake; hence the legend of the serpent guarding the golden apples in the garden of the Hesperides;

Alligator is the Spanish el lagarto (Latin lacertus), a lizard;

Daffodil should be affodil, a form of asphodel; tansy is the French athanasie;

Omelette is the French l'alemette, a cake.

Many words have been so long popularly mis-spelled that the error has become fastened to the language:

Sound should be soun (as if we said gownd for gown);

Sovereign should be sovran, and foreign, forein;

Scapoy should be Sepoy (for the Oriental Sipahi, a
  soldier) ;

Sirloin should be sur-loin (the part above the loin) ;

Sirname should be surname ;

Rhyme has no right to the " h ; " it should be rime ;

There should be no " l " in could ;

Frontispiece should be frontispice, from the Latin
  frontispicium, the front seen (of a building) ;

Guarantee should be guaranty, and repartee should
  be reparty ;

We object to any one pronouncing real, reel ; but
  ordeal should be ordeel, for it means an out-
  deal ;

Dragomen for Dragomans. He travelled in the
  East with two *Dragomen*. The correct plural
  forms of Dragoman, Turcoman, and Ottoman
  end in s. Yet these endings are not analogous: in Dragoman the suffix an is simply
  adjectival ; in Turcoman (properly Turkmân)
  the ending mân is a Persian word meaning
  like or *thus*, Turkmân really meaning Turk-
  like ; and Ottoman (properly Uthmân) is simply a proper noun wrongly used in an adjectival
  sense ;

It is a mistake to use aborigine as the singular
  number of aborigines. Alms is really a singular word, though now used in the plural ; and
  news is properly used by Shakespeare with
  these (" Wherefore should these good news
  make me sick ? " " 2 Henry IV.," IV., 2), though

now we use it as if it were a singular word made up of the points of the compass, N., E., W., S. Assets should properly be singular; bellows and gallows, plurals; eaves is singular, and its proper plural is eaveses, though custom has dropped it. So riches is the French *richesse*, and is really singular; summons is the French *semonce*, a citation.

CHAPTER XIV.

MISTAKEN DERIVATIONS.

Philomel. — This word for the nightingale, so affected by early English poets, is not derived from the Greek words meaning melody-loving, but from phileo and mèlon, fruit lovers. The gale in nightingale has nothing to do with the wind, but is allied to our yell; it is therefore the nightsinger.

The word honeymoon has no connection with honey other than in the fact that its Icelandic congener *hjon*, "a wedded pair," may be related to the Anglo-Saxon *hiwa*, a hive, or *hiv*, a house.

Unruly has Nothing to do with Rules. — The translators of the Bible and many other writers have naturally connected unruly with rule, as in the phrase "Warn them that are unruly" when the marginal reading is "disorderly." But unruly corresponds to the German *unruhig*, restless, and is not allied to rule.

A Brown Study under a Different Color. — When we find a friend in a brown study we remark on it and wonder what is the color of his thoughts. They may be blue, but not brown. It may be a perversion of the old French *embronc*, which means bound down, sad, pensive, thoughtful, allied to *prone*.

Bucks and Bulls. — The animal kingdom is not responsible for buckwheat. Buck is another form of beech, and it is really beech-wheat, so called because of the resemblance of the kernels to beech-nuts. Neither has a papal bull nor an Irish bull any connection with the fierce lord of the field. The one is from the Latin *bulla*, a seal, the other from the Icelandic *bull*, nonsense. On the other hand, the disreputable verb *cabbage* is not really a slander on the vegetable. It comes from the Dutch *Kabassen*, to steal, to bag, to put in one's basket, *Kabas*.

Carnival. — Byron, in "Beppo," says:

> " This fast is named the Carnival, which being
> Interpreted implies ' farewell to flesh ; '
> So called because, the name and thing agreeing,
> Through Lent they live on fish both salt and fresh."

But Byron was wrong. Carnival is not from the Latin *caro* and *vale*, but from Low Latin *carne-levamen*, a consolation of the flesh.

Helpmeet or Helpmate. — In Genesis II., 18, it says: "I will make him an help meet [that is, fit] for him." This collation of noun and adjective has been welded into a common noun. But the real compound should be help-mate.

The Peep o' Day is the Pipe o' Day. — Children at least suppose that the expression peep o' day refers to day peeping or peering over the eastern horizon. Palsgrave in 1530 gives the true meaning, " at daye pype," " *à la pipe du jour* ; " that is, the time when the birds begin to sing — "the earliest pipe of half-awakened birds."

Pennyroyal worth More than a Penny. — An old-fashioned remedy is "pennyrile tea." The word is a corruption of the translation of the botanical name pulegium regium, pulege, puliall royal, hence pennyroyal.

Penthouse. — There is no house to a penthouse except the house to which it is appended. The word is really pentice, from the Latin *pendere*, to hang. It was an over-refinement that lengthened it into its present form.

Philopena or Philippine. — The game of forfeit called by Americans philopena, as it is a penalty of love is supposed to be derived from the German Vielliebchen corrupted into Philippinchen, a sweetheart or valentine.

Pickaxes. — There is no axe about a pickaxe. The genuine English word is pickeys, a pick, sometimes spelt pycoyse.

Pile. — Wordsworth begins his elegiac stanzas suggested by a picture of Peel Castle with the line,

"I was thy neighbor once, thou rugged pile."

He probably did not realize that he was making a pun. Pile and peel are the same word, meaning castle. The word pile for a wooden stake comes from the Latin *pila*, a pier or pillar; pile, a heap, from the Latin *pila*, a ball.

The Milliner and the Million. — The word milliner is sometimes supposed to be derived from the Latin *mille*, a thousand, as of one that dealt in the thousand and one articles of feminine dress-ornamentation. It is really from Milaner, a person that sold gloves, laces, and other finery from Milan. But the word tureen is not derived from Turin; it is for terrine, made of earth (*terra*). Bartlett says that million for melon is an old corruption of melon, and Colgrave is quoted as giving countenance to it. Du Bartas in 1621 speaks of the marine "vines, roses, nettles, millions, pinks, gilliflowers, mushrooms."

Vinegar's Mother. — Probably most persons imagine that there is a maternal relationship between vinegar and its mother. The word is really mudder, which is found in all Germanic languages, with the natural sense of mud, thickening.

Running a-muck. — There is no relationship between Bunyan's man with the muck-rake and Dryden's man who " runs an Indian muck at all he meets." The word is derived from the Malasian *amok*, signifying a peculiar frenzy which sometimes impels the native to rush into a crowd, striking blindly with his *kris* or crease. McNair, in his " Perak and the Malays," says: " The first warning of such an event is given by the cry '*Amok, amok*,' when there is a rush, and people fly right and left to shelter." And in " Tavernier's Voyages " (II., p. 202) it says: " Drawing their poisoned daggers, they cried a mocca upon the English."

Welcome is not Well Come. — Welcome is not an English translation of the Italian *ben-venuto*, well and come, but is a corruption of Anglo-Saxon *wil-cuma*, from *wil*, gladly, and *cumian*, to receive; hence an acceptable guest.

Rabbits and Rarebits. — Archbishop Trench asserts that in the dish of melted cheese the word rabbit is a corruption of rarebit. Palmer says it is really rabbit, "the mock heroes of the eating-house," like "Irish apricots," for potatoes; "Cape Cod turkeys," for codfish; "Digby chickens," for herring; "Albany beef," for sturgeon; and the like. A Frenchman translated it as *un lapin du pays de Galles!*

Whaling for Wailing. — Jamieson, in his Scotch dictionary, quotes this definition of whaling: "a lashing with a rope's end, from the name of a rope called a whale-line, used in fishing for whales." It should be wale, or welt.

Whiskey and Water. — Whiskey, which used to be spelt usquebaugh, comes from the Keltic *uisge*, which means water. It is the same word that is found in many English names of localities, the *Wash*, *Usk*, *Ox*-ford, *Ex*-mouth, *Ouse*, *Isis*, like the Indian termination *eg*, *og*, *ock*, *unk*, which also means water. It is ingeniously hidden in the name of Phœnix Park, Dublin, which was really Fionn-uisg, clear spring, but a column in the park shows a phœnix rising from a pyre.

Acres and Wiseacres. — When a dull lawyer

argued that none should be admitted to the bar except those that had some landed property, Curran said: "May I ask, sir, how many acres make a wise-acre?" But the word is another form of the German *Weissager*, wise-sayer, or wizard. On the other hand, the word witch in witch-hazel is not connected except in imagination with the power of the tree in detecting water. It is the wicken or wick-tree; in Anglo-Saxon cwic-brain, which means living tree.

Woman Woe to Man. — It used to be thought seriously that the word woman meant woe to men, "Because by woman," says Southey, "was woe brought into the world." Of course that is false etymology; nor is the derivation from womb and man any more accurate. It is from *wif*, the weaver, or possibly from the Anglo-Saxon *wifan*, to join or weave together, the *conjunx*, the joined-to-man.

One who Muses does not necessarily cultivate the Muses. — This word does not come from the muses, but is from the French *muser*, which is a term of the chase meaning to lift the muzzle into the air and stand as if listening, pausing, or pondering.

The Old Nick. — Some persons confuse the name Nicholas with the popular name of the Evil One. Thus Butler in "Hudibras" says that Niccolò Machiavelli "gave his name to our Old Nick;" and in one of Ramsay's poems it appears as Auld Nicol. But the term is a relic of the old English *nicor*, a goblin, allied to the word nixy. Palmer says that Old Harry was originally used in reference to Henry's destruction of the monasteries. It might be confused with the verb harry, to lay waste.

Or Ever. — In the authorized version of Daniel it says, "The lions had the mastery of them and brake all their bones or ever they came at the bottom of the den." Here the translators imagined that ever, of which e'er is a contraction, was a more dignified form than *ere* or *or* alone. Or ere is tautological.

Pagoda. — Bailey, in his dictionary, derives pagoda from Pagan's god. It may be derived from the Persian but-khodà, Idol-God.

Pea-Jacket. — Captain Marryat, in "Poor Jack," says that the article of sea-apparel called P-jacket got its name as an abbreviation of pilot-jacket. But the pea part is evidently from the old English *py*, a cloak, as in court-py. The Dutch word *pij* means a rough coat.

Marbles not made of Marble. — As marbles are never made of marble, the origin of the word by which boys call the little round balls in their game must probably be sought elsewhere. In Evans' glossary it is explained as a term manufactured from *marl*, out of which in some parts of England marbles are made. Palmer derives the name from the French *marelles*.

Nightmares. — Captain Burton, in "Etruscan

Bologna," confounded the ending mare in night-mare with the female of the horse, and the illustrator Fuseli depicted the incubus as visiting a sleeper in the shape of a snarling mare. With the same mistaken notion Shakespeare, in "King Lear" (III., 4), speaks of "the nightmare and her nine foals." Sir Walter Scott, Charles Lamb, and many other writers have been likewise deceived. The word is really the Anglo-Saxon *mara*, allied to the Sanskrit *mara*, a devil or destroyer.

Jerked Meat. — What most persons imagine to be the significance of jerked in the compound "jerked beef" it would be hard to say. The word is not derived from the verb to jerk, but from the Peruvian *charki*, as is shown by the following citation from Prescott's "Conquest of Peru": "Flesh cut into thin slices was distributed among the people, who converted it into *charki*, the dried meat of the country."

An Ark that was not Noah's. — It is a mistake to suppose that the word *ark*, often used in the sense of citadel, especially in regard to oriental or Indian towns, is derived from the Latin *arx*, though it may have the same root as seen in *arceo*, to keep off, defend. It is a genuine Persian word, properly spelt *arg*.

Belfries and Bells. — A belfry is not necessarily a tower to hold a bell. We are misled by the sound. It is the English form of the French *beffroi*, and was often spelt berfray or bewfray, a watch-tower.

The Bitter End. — We sometimes speak of carrying a feud out to the bitter end, and suppose that it is the same word as used in the phrase " a bitter disappointment." It was, however, originally a nautical term. The bitter's end is that part of the cable that, being coiled around the *bites* or bitts, remains on board. Admiral Smyth is quoted as saying, in " The Sailor's Word Book ": " When a chain or rope is paid out to the bitter end, no more remains to be let go."

Bonfires not Bonefires. — Dr. Johnson, in his dictionary, says that bonfire is a fire made on the receipt of good news. Other earlier lexicographers thought it was so called because it was made of " clear bones and no woode " (Fuller, " Mixt Contemplation "). Shakespeare, in " Macbeth," speaks of " the everlasting bonfire," as if for bale-fire, a funeral pyre.

The Heir Apparent. — The word *apparent* in the expression " heir apparent " is derived either from paraunt, for paravaunt, meaning first, or else from *apparenté*, related.

Various Mistakes in Derivations. — Apple-pie order is not an order peculiar to the region of perpetual pie. It is from *cap à pie*, referring to the complete equipment of a soldier. Neither has the word attic anything to do with Greece. Palmer says it is a word borrowed from the Sanskrit " *attak*," the top room in an Indian house. Veranda also may be from the Sanskrit direct through the Portuguese.

Carryall, the name of the American carriage, is not so called because it conveys the whole family, but it is a corruption of the French *cariole*.

The plant that country folk call *cast-me-down* or stickadove is a curious metamorphosis of the botanical name cassidone, which is derived from *Stoechas Sidonia*.

Cat's cradle has nothing to do with cats. The word is a perversion of *cratch* (French *crèche*), a wicker-work rack.

Nor is catsup in any sense a dish to set before Tabby. It is the English spelling of the Indian word *kitjap*.

The Italian word *cento*, as in a *cento* of verses, is not derived from *centum*, a hundred, but from the Greek *kentrôn*, a patch-work.

The old-fashioned stock in trade of the novelists was a changeling, but it is a mistake to suppose it meant originally one child *changed* for another in the cradle; it is derived from old English chang (kang), an idiot, a natural; such children were popularly supposed to be brought by the fairies and substituted for the bright baby born. "Such men do chaungelings call so chaunged by Fairies' theft," says Spenser.

A cutlet is not a little cut, any more than a bullet is a little bull. It is derived from the French *côtelette*, and means a rib (*côte*) of any kind of animal.

More Examples. — The old English cloth called ciprus, cyprus, cipres, or "cobweb lawne," derives its names probably with the French *crêpe*, from the Latin *crispus, curled* linen. Connected with the idea of mourning, it naturally took the form of cypress; as where Jeremy Taylor speaks of " black cypress, a veil of penitential sorrow."

Many poets think there is a verb to darkle, to rhyme conveniently with sparkle. But the word darkling is not a present participle; it is an adverb meaning " in the dark." " Out went the candle and we were left darkling," says Shakespeare (" King Lear," I., 4).

Davy Jones' Locker is supposed to have a biblical original, Jones standing for Jonah, and David, a popular nautical name, being prefixed.

Demijohn has nothing to do with the John which stands as the typical name of all nations (John Bull, Jean Crapaud, Hans, Ivan, Johnnie Reb, etc.). Damajana is a large glass bottle; the French make it *dame-jeanne;* the Italians, *damigiana.* Of course it is possible that the Arabic is derived from the French; though Littré's dictionary connects the ending with Turkish *jouna,* a glass bottle.

Charles's Wain.—Tennyson speaks of Charles's Wain in " The May Queen." Who was the Charles thus apotheosized and put into the sky like an ancient hero? Charlemagne? Some have thought so, others have attributed the honor to Charles I. or II. But it is really the churl's wain or farmer's wagon; just as the Greeks called it *hámaxa,* a chariot. Neither is Charlotte Russe named after a hypothetical

Russian woman, *tsaritsa* or peasant; it comes from the old English charlet, which is in turn derived from the French *chair*, meat.

Chicken-hearted Cowards. — Chicken-hearted does injustice to the domestic fowl, which is generally a doughty fighter. The word is connected with Swedish *kikna*, to lose heart; and has several congeners in the English dialect. Neither has coward (cowheart) anything to do with the domestic cow, or with cowherd as Spenser spells it. The timid hare is conart (equal to short-tail). The connection is evident, then, with the word tail.

Milk and Wine. — Clouted cream is a corruption of clotted cream. The Rev. A. S. Palmer points out the fact that clouted means nailed, and that the Greek words for to fix and to nail were likewise applied to curdled milk. Our fathers in the old intemperate days liked mulled wine. Mulled is not really from a verb, but from mould, earth, and signifies the wine used at the *molde ealu*, or funeral feast.

Discords in the Heart. — It is a mistake to think that when you hear a discord the word cord is necessarily involved. It comes from *dis*, apart, and *cors*, heart; hearts at variance; so with accordance, concord.

Asses and Dogs and Frogs. — Some persons imagine that a painter's easel is so called because it makes his work easier. It is from the Latin *asellus*, a little ass, and is therefore of the same breed

as our clothes-horse.   In the same way pulley is
not from the verb to pull, but from pulain, a colt.

In the word grayhound the color of the dog does
not give it the name.   It is really the Graian or
Grecian dog, as Spaniel is the Spanish dog.

The term curmudgeon is not derived from any
reference to " puppy, whelp, or hound, or cur of low
degree."   It is for cornmudgin or corn dealer,
corn-hoarder; hence parsimonious.   The word cor-
morant is allied with it, as corn-vorant; neither is
the dog-fish so called because it is fond of *dogs*; it
is really the dag or dagger fish.

When, some time since, two railway companies
quarrelled over a crossing, and the employees of
the one pulled up the newly laid rails and frogs
of the other, a wit called the contest " a new
batrachiomachia, or battle of the frogs."   The word
frog in such a connection or as applied to a part of
a horse's hoof is a corruption of *frush*, for fursh, a
fork (Latin *furca*).   But a frog on a coat is a frock
ornament.

Persons who live in " flats " imagine that the
name is given to their apartments because the
rooms are all on one floor.   But it is derived from
the Anglo-Saxon *flett*, a dwelling, house, or chamber.   In Scotch *flet* is a floor or story of a house.

It is a mistake to imagine the Freemasons are
any more free than those that do not belong to the
order.   Schele de Vere derives the term from
Frère-Mason, a brother mason.

Puzzles for Foreigners. — A stranger in the Boston post-office asked a man whom he met, " Where is the *foragin* office ? " He made a mistake in pronunciation (though perhaps not far from the truth) ; but the g in foreign is a mistake. It is an interloper ; Chaucer spelt it forayn. It comes from the Latin *foris*, out of doors. It should be properly spelt foren or forein.

Nothing puzzles a *forener* more than the pronunciation of our English words ending in ough. The Frenchman who said he had a cow in his box may have studied Wright's " Fifteenth Century Vocabularies," where *hic tusses* is translated as the *cowe*. Bethought is still pronounced bethoft in some parts of England, and daughter as dafter. The soldier's leave of absence is a corruption of the Dutch *ver-lof* (German *Verlaub*) (*lof, laub*, and *leave* being identical in meaning), and was originally called furlof.

Gaits and Shoes. — When a boy wants to make sport of a companion he often says he " has a gait like a pair of bars." The pun really recalls the old spelling, which is correct. Gait has no near connection with " go." It is the same as the Swedish *gata* or *gatan*, and means a road or street. To " gang your ain gait" is to go your own way. A secondary meaning crept in, and the word now means a mode of walking. The same word is compounded with lope, to run, in the expression to run the gantlope, or incorrectly the *gauntlet;* that is, to run through a lane or street of soldiers each armed with whips. Some people imagine the word galoshes is derived from gallo-shoes, as if of French origin. It is supposed by most etymologists to come through the Latin colopedia, a wooden shoe, from the Greek *kalo-pedion* — a " wood foot " or last. Now it is used in all countries for rubber overshoes, as for instance *galoshi*, in Russia.

Hessian boots are not boots worn by Hessians, but boots and gaiters in one, from the old word *huseons*, which is perhaps the same as the English diminutive hos-kins, little hose.

Gambrel-roofs. — Dr. Holmes, in a quatrain, describes the origin of the word gambrel-roof :

" Gambrel, gambrel, let me beg
   You'll look at a horse's hinder leg ;
   First great angle above the hoof,
   That is the gambrel ; hence gambrel roof."

Gambrel is a cant term for a crooked stick. It is derived from the Welsh and Irish cam; Indo-European root *gam*, meaning crooked. When Scott speaks of the devil's *game* leg he means a crooked, a disabled leg ; when a lamb gambols it plays with its legs, and yet the word has no connection with *game*. A gammon (or wrongly spelt gambone) of bacon is from the same root, as is also ham.

Modified Oaths. — Many persons wishing to express their feelings, but not wishing openly to break the commandment, use modified oaths as if they were more harmless. Oh, dear, is the French

O Dieu; Jiminy is either the Latin *Gemini* (Castor and Pollux), or else *O Jesu Domine*; la or law is for Lord; gosh is for God; zounds is for God's wounds; Od'sbodkins is God's body; Od'spitikins, God's pity.

Different Kinds of Gin. — Gin is sometimes called Geneva, as if it were a distinctively Swiss drink. But the liquor is made from the juniper, which in French is *giniévre*.

Victor Hugo wrote a curious poem called " Les Djinns." All readers of the Arabian Nights are acquainted with the powerful spirits called Jin or Genies. The word is allied with the Latin *Genius*, but comes from the Persian *Jinni* (plural *Jin*).

Instep. — It is a curious, but natural, mistake to connect that part of the foot called the instep with step. Skeat's dictionary says it is from in and stoop, the in-bend of the foot.

Isinglass. — The thin sheets of transparent or translucent mica, and the gelatine used in making jelly, sometimes misspelled icing-glass, get their name from the Dutch *huyzenblas*, which means sturgeon bladder. The spelling *icing* seems to have arisen from the original meaning of jelly (French *gélée*), something frozen.

Jackalls and Jackstones. — The popularity of the name John and its variant Jack is also seen in the word jackall or jack-call, which is really the Persian *shaghal*, the howler, and in *jackstones*, which should be chack or chuck-stones.

Jolly-boats. — Few persons when they read in nautical novels of the captain going ashore in the jolly-boat realize that it is only another name for the yawl, the yawly-boat.

In the Soup. — When we have our first course of soup and call for Julienne we little think of the strange origin of the word. It used to be made with sorrel, the name of which in Italy is *alleluia*, because its ternate leaf was regarded as an emblem of the trinity. The soup was introduced into France by the Italian cooks of Catherine de' Medici, under the name *juliola*. Hence Julienne! Neither is a *purée* soup a pure soup. It comes from the old English and French *porée*, a vegetable pottage, from the Latin *porrum*, a leek, *porrata*, leek soups.

Against the Grain. — When one speaks of something going "against the grain," the picture suggested is of a knife or plane running in opposition to the fibres of the wood; it is a popular and effective metaphor; but in old times, when French had a greater influence on the language than it has now, we find it expressed "against the *gré* or *gree*;" that is, against the wish or desire.

Grass Widows. — A grass widow is generally regarded as a woman whose husband has gone to grass. Some writers try to find an explanation in the French *grace*, a widow by courtesy. As it is grass in the Scandinavian languages, others have conjectured that it comes from the word *gradig* (our greedy), signifying a woman who longs for her husband. Here one may have a wide choice.

It is generally supposed that the word great in the expression "they are great friends" is almost slang, like "thick." But it is commonly used by early writers, often alone. Pepys, in his "Diary," says: "Lady Castlemare is still great with the king." Bishop Hall says: "Moses was great with God." It has been derived in this connection from the Irish *gradh*, dear; from the Anglo-Saxon *grétan*, to know familiarly, our greet.

It is a mistake to suppose that the broad, short, crooked sword commonly used in the Middle Ages, and called *hanger*, was so called because it hung by the side. The name is a corruption of the Arabic and Persian *khanjar*, a sabre. In the French it also appears with the article *al alfange*. Neither has the word hangnail anything to do with *hang*; it is in Old English *agnel*, and may derive from ange, pain.

Husband is not a house band, but simply the house master, *band* in the compound being the teller or owner.

Sleepers that do not wake. — The word sleeper has been ingeniously connected in relationship with dormer, as in dormer-window. It is really another form of the Norwegian *sleip*, meaning slippery, hence a smooth piece of wood, and comparable with slab and slipper.

The word vent, for a small opening, has no more

to do with the Latin *ventus*, the wind, than the word door has to do with *window*, as Webster says. It is another form of *fent*, a cleft or chink (just as vixen is the feminine of fox).

Pudding should have no " g."—When children leave the " g " off from pudding they really make no mistake. It was added by a refinement of affected gentility, just as some persons now say capting for captain, chicking for chicken, kitching for kitchen, woolling for woollen.

A Quarry, but not of Rock. — In reading English books where hunting terms are introduced, many persons mistake the word quarry, used for game. It comes from the Latin *cor*, the heart, and originally signified the part of the intestines given the dogs as a reward for good work; the corresponding French term is *corée*.

The Reindeer. — The introduction of the reindeer into the Klondyke has caused various newspaper writers to speak of the animal as if it derived its name from the word *rein*, because it is harnessed. There is some doubt as to the real origin of the term, but there is no doubt that reins as " lines " must be ruled out. The German for it is *Rennthier*, " a beast that runs." Others derive it from the Lapp *reino*, a posture, hence the domesticated deer. In Icelandic it is called *hreinn*, clean.

Ridings are Thirdings. — Palmer says that rook, the name of the castle in the game of chess, is a corruption of Italian *rocco*, a fort or castle, which in turn is a corruption of the Persian *rokh*, a boat, that being the original form of the piece. But in Persian the term is *rukh*, and means cheek.

Shrubs that do not Grow. — Shrub in the expression raspberry shrub is the same term as sirop and sherbet, which in turn are derived from the Arabic *sharib*, to drink.

Steelyard. — One of the oddest of popular misunderstandings of words is steelyard, which has neither steel nor yard in its makeup. It is a corruption of stelleere, or steller, a regulator or balance.

Tailors and Hatters. — The common slur on tailors, that nine tailors make a man, is said to be derived from the practice of tolling the bell thrice three times for the death of a man, and twice three times for the death of a woman. Hence nine *tellers* made it a man. In the same way the idea that hatters have a traditionally hot temper arises from the old English word hetter meaning furious, raging; so that "as mad as a hatter" is easily explained.

Names of People and Places. — On the authority of Monier Williams, the name of that great prophet usually called "Mahomet" ought to be spelt thus, "Muhammad," this being the passive participle of the verb *hamada*, signifying "to praise." The original family name, as given by Lake, was Kothan. "There is certainly not more than one with a more interesting career than

Mahomet, or, more correctly, Muhammad," says the "Daily Chronicle."

"Bede" is the common way of spelling the name of "The father of English learning." The correct way is Bæda.

Also Swithhun — which is the form given in our native manuscripts — is not only turned into Swithun, with one "h," rendering the word meaningless, but is even changed into Swithin. And the Christian name of the celebrated architect, Inigo Jones, would, if properly spelt, be Enego.

The correct pronunciation of Pepys, as given by a descendant of the Diarist, is not, as usually heard, "Peps," but *Peeps*, as *Weems* for Wemys. The common way of saying "dahlia," as if *daylia*, is really naming a totally different plant, — the "dalea," — a greenhouse perennial named after the English botanist, Dr. Samuel Dale, whereas the "dahlia" was named after the Swedish botanist Dahl.

Proper names Misapplied. — The name of Tom, popularly applied to bells, is derived from the boom of the bell-tone, as in tom-tom. The terms Cicely and Alison are not used in connection with sweet feminine proper names. Sweet Cicily is the Greek Sesilis; Sweet Alison is alyssum. Valentine's day is not a saint's day. Valentine comes from *galantine*, a lover. But as birds pair about the time of Bishop Valentine's martyrdom,

February 14, that day was used as a popular time for love missives, and called Valentine.

Nor is Will in Will o' the Wisp a proper name; it is the same as the Icelandic *villa*, to bewilder.

Trifles. — Trivial and trifle are not allied. The meaning of trifle would seem to connect it with trivial; but they are drawn from sources far apart. Trivial is from a Latin word meaning cross-roads, and hence popular, common, and finally cheap. Trifle is a jest or lying story, from the French *truffer*, to mock.

CHAPTER XV.

MISTAKES IN SPEAKING AND WRITING.

High-pitched Voices. — It is a common mistake, especially in New England and among women, to speak in a high and artificial voice. The nasal quality that makes our American voices so disagreeable may with care be overcome. Speak low and distinctly.

Hesitation in Speech. — Language is a tool. It should be used with skill. Notice how many speakers, both in public and in private, hesitate and stammer. It is a mistake to prefix or add the gliding syllables *er* or *a* to a word. It is unnecessary; it is a bad habit; but it may be cured.

Use of Slang. — It is a mistake to use slang or to pepper one's speech with expletives. All extravagance in language weakens the effect. It is a mistake to qualify every verb and adjective with "awfully." Even the example of Plato does not make it advisable.

Conceit. — Conceit is odious. It is generally a mistake to talk about one's self. More interesting topics may be easily found.

Mispronunciations. — Most of us pronounce our own language inaccurately. In the majority of words there is authority for several pronunciations. Then we may take our choice. A list of the commonest mistakes is here appended.

Do not pronounce:

*Ab*domen for ab*do*men;
*Ac*climate for ac*cli*mate;
*A*keret for *accu*rate;
*A*crost for across;
*A*cumen for ac*u*men;
Admir*alty* for ad*mi*ralty;
*Ad*ult for ad*ult;*
Ad*verse* for ad*v*erse;
A*gain* for ag*ĕn;*
Ag*gran*dize for *ag*gran-dize;
*Ā*gil for *ă*gil;
Agriculturalist for agri-*cult*urist;
Ala*bas*ter for *al*abaster;
*Al*bumen for al*bu*men;
A*li*as for *al*ias;
*Al*legro for al*le*gro;
Alle*pathy* for al*lo*pathy;
*Al*lȳ for al*ly;*
*Al*mond for ahmond;
*A*lms for ahmz;
*A*mature for amateur;
A*me*nable for a*me*nable;
A*me*nity for a*me*nity;
An' for and;

*An*cient for ainshent;
Annilate for an*ni*hilate;
Anti*podes* for an*ti*pŏdēs;
*A*pex for *ă*pex;
Apotheosis for apo*the*o-sis; •
Ap*pā*rent for appairent;
*A*pricot for *a*pricot;
*A*rab for *A*rab;
Arch-etect for arketect;
*A*rtic for Arctic;
*A*rea for *a*rea;
*A*reola for ar*e*ola;
Ar*kan*sas for *Ark*-an-saw;
(Arquebus) *a*rkebuse for ark-we-bus;
Sparrowgrass for as*par*-agus;
*A*spirant·for as*pi*rant;
A*the*neum for Athe*ne*um;
Au*da*shus for au*da*cious;
*Au*reola for au*reo*la;
*A*venoo for avenue;
*A*von for *A*-von;
*Aw*fl for awful;

(Bacillus) *basillus* for ba-*cil*-lus.

(Bade) bāde for *băd*;

Ban*ana* for ban*ah*na;

Bah relief for bass relief;

(Been) bēēn for *bin*;

Be*h*emoth for *b*ehemoth;

Be*l*ial for *B*elial;

(Bicycle) bicycl for *bi*cicl;

*Bit*umen for bi*tu*men;

Blas*ph*emious for *blas*phe-mous;

Black-guard for *blăg*gard;

Boatswain for *bōsn*;

*Bun*net for bŏnnet;

Bowsprit for *bōs*prit;

*Br*ig*and* for *brig*and;

(Buoy) boy for *booee*;

Callio*pe* for cal-*li*-op-e;

(Calm) cam for cahm;

Cam*el*-*leop*ard for cam*el*opard;

Cam*f*ire for camphor;

(Caoutchouc) c a t h - ōō-chuk for kōōchōōk;

*Ca*pillary for *Ca*pillary;

Cari*b*bean for Cari*b*bean;

*C*arotid for ca-*rot*-id;

*C*atridge for cartridge;

Cas*tell*an for *cast*ellan;

Cas-tle for cas'l;

Cau*cas*us for *Cau*casus;

(Chasten) chäsn for chāsn;

(Chicago) Chica*h*go for Chicawgo;

Childern for children;

Chi*val*rous for *shi*valrous;

(Cinchona) sin*ch*ona for sin*k*ōna;

(Cocheneal) *Coach*eneal for *colch*eneal;

Cockatrise for cock-a-trice (tris);

*C*ognomen for cog*n*omen;

(Column) colyum for *col*um;

(Comely) comb-ly for cumly;

Com*p*arable for *com*parable;

Com*p*rom*i*se for *com*promize;

Conch for *konk*;

Con*d*olence for con*do*lence;

*Con*fiscate for con*fis*cate;
Consid*able* for consid-
erable;
Con*spir*acy for con*spir*-
acy
Con*trary* for *contrary*;
*Cŏr*al for *coral*;
Counsl for counsel;
Coverlid for coverlet;
Coward*ice* for *cowardis*;
*Cram*berry for cran-
berry;
Crik for creek;
*Crem*atory for *crem*-a-
tory;
Crinoline for crinolin;
*Cul*inary for *cu*-linary;
Cupalo for cupola;
(Curaçao) *Kew-ra-soar*
for *Kŏŏ-ra-só*;
(Curtain) *curtn* for
curtin;
Cyc*lo*pean for cyc*lo*pean;
Dandeline for dandelion;
Dan-ish for *Danish*;
Daylia for dah-lia;
Deaf (deef) for def;
Debenture for de-*bent*-
ure;
Decade for *decade*;

Decadence for deca-
dence;
Decorative for *decora*-
tive;
Decorous for decorous;
Decreped for decrepit;
De-*line-itive* for *defini*-
tive;
Dĕpo for station;
Derilic for der*elict*;
Dezolate for desolate;
(Desuetude) desooetood
for *des*wetude;
Devastate for *devastate*;
Doo for dew;
Direc'ly for derectly;
Dis*put*ant for dis*put*ant;
(Docile) do-sil or dō-sile
for *dos*-sil;
Dolorous for *dolorous*;
Do-ric for dor-ic.
(Dromedary) *dromedary*
for *drum*edary.
Doo for due or dew; or
du for do.
(Dubious) doobious for
dewbious;
Dook for duke;
Dinasty for *dynasty*;
Effut for effort;

E*lig*ible for *el*igible ;
Elum for elm ; .
*Ele*cution for *elo*cution ;
*Ae*neid for Aeneid ;
(Engine) enjine for en-
jĭn ;
(English) English for
Inglish ;
*E*nsilage for en-*sigh*-
lage ;
Enth*oo*siasm for enthusi-
asm ;
(Epaulet) epulet for *epo*-
let ;
(Epistle) e-*pistl* for episl ;
(Equitable) *equi*tabl for
*ek*witable ;
Er-*a*-to for *Er*-ato ;
*I*rysipilus for *e*resypilas ;
Es*p*ionage for *e*spionage ;
Eu*ro*pean for Euro*p*ean ;
Eu*ride*ice for Eu-*ryd*-i-ce ;
Evenin for evening ;
Evry for *ev*ery ;
(Evil) eve-il for ĕvl ;
(Excursion) excurzhun
for excurshun ;
Exemplar for egzemplar ;
Ex*pa*triate for ex*pa*tri-
ate ;

Ex*pli*cable for *ex*plic-
able ;
Ex*qui*zit for *ex*quisite ;
Extry for extra ;
(Extraordinary) extra-
ordinary for extrordi-
nary ;
Fairenheet for Fahr-en-
heit ;
*Fan*atic for fa-*nat*ic ;
Fasset for faucet ;
Fav*orite* for favorit ;
(February) Febuary for
Febrooary ;
*F*ecund for *fe*cund ;
Fellah for fellow ;
(Feminine) feminine for
feminin ;
(Fertile) fertile for *fertil* ;
Fi-delity for fid-elity ;
Figger for figure ;
Filum for film ;
(Finale) fin-*ale* for fin-
ah-le ;
(Flaccid) flassid for flak-
sid ;
Forehead for *for-ed* ;
Forgit for forget ;
For*mid*able for *formid*-
able ;

Fortnit for fortnight;

Frag*men*tary for frag-mentary;

*Frun*tispiece for frontispiece;

*Ful*crum for fulcrum;

(Furniture) furnichewer for *fur*-nit-yur;

Futile for *futil*;

(Gasoline) gasoleen for *gaso*lin;

(Gauntlet) gawntlet for gahntlet;

*Gen*rully or gen-ally for *generally*;

(Genuine) genu*ine* for genuin;

(Gerund) *jer*und for *jer*und;

Gist for *jist*;

Git for get;

Gladi*o*lus for gladi*o*lus;

God-iva for Go-*di*-va;

Golden for goldn;

Gondola for gon*d*ola;

Gor-illa for go-rilla;

Govermunt for *gov*-ern-ment;

Gra-nery for gran-ery;

Grat-is for gra-tis;

Grev-i-ous for griev-ous;

*Grim*ace for grim*ace*;

Grim-aulkin for gri-*mal*-kin;

Gardeen for guardian;

Hāst-en for *hā̇sn*;

Helum for helm;

Hercu*le*an for hercu*le*an;

Hibernate for *hi*bernate;

*Hir*oglyphic for hi-er-o-glyph-ic;

Ho-lo-caust for *hol*-o-caust;

Hor-i-zon for ho-*ri*-zon;

Hō-ro-scope for *hor*-o-scope;

Hos-*pit*-able for *hos*-pit-a-ble;

(Hough) huf for hok;

Hung for hanged (of criminals);

*Hymen*eal for hymen*e*al;

Hi-poc-risy for hyp-ocrisy;

(Ichneumon)*itch-neumon* for *iknumon*;

*I*dea for idea;

I-deel for i-*de*-al.

Id-yl for *i*-dyl;

*I*llustrate for il*lus*trate;

Imm*e*jetly for im-*me*-di-ate-ly;

Im*pi*ously for *imp*-i-ously;

Im-*plac*-able for im-*pla*-cable;

Inaugerate for inaug-u-rate;

In-com-*par*-able for in-*com*parable;

In-cor-po-ral for in-cor-*po*-re-al;

In-*dec*-o-rous for in-de-*co*-rous;

In-*dus*-try for *in*-dus-try;

In*ex*-o-rable for in-*ex*-orable;

In*ex*plic*-able for in-*ex*-plic-a-ble;

In-hos*pi*table for in*hos*-pitable;

(Inmost) in-must for *in*-mŏst;

*In*quiry for in-*qui*-ry;

Insex for insects;

In*sidu*-ous for in-sid-i-ous;

In-*te*-gral for *in*-te-gral;

Inter*es*ting for *in*terest-ing;

In-ter-locutor for inter-*locutor*;

In-test-ine for *in*-*test-in*;

*In*trigue for int*rigue*;

(Invalide) *in*-va-*leed* for in-va-lid;

(Inveigle) in-*vā*-gl for in-*vec*-gl;

In*ven*tory for *in*-ven-to-ry;

I-*rash*-able for i-*ras*-ci-ble;

(Iron) i-ron for *iurn*;

Ir-re*par*-able for ir*rep*-arable;

Irre*vo*cable for ir*rev*-o-cable;

Eye-talian for It-al-ian;

I-vry for ivory;

Gen-u-ary for Jăn-u-ary;

Jeopardize for jeopard;

Jeru*zalem* for Jerusa-lem;

(Jewel) *jule* for ju-el;

(Jowl) jowl for *jōle*;

Jug-ular for ju-gular;

Ketch for catch;

Ketchn or *kitchn* for kitchen;

Kittle for kettle;

(Kiln) kiln for *kil*;

Labl for *la*-bel;

Labrer for laborer;

La-conism for *lac*-o-nism;

Ladoga for *Lad*-o-ga;

(Landau) lander or lan-do for *lan-daw*;

Lap-el for la-*pel*;

*Lat*ent for *la*-tent;

Latn for Lat-in;

(Laundress) *lawndress* for *lahndress*;

(Leisure) lezh-ur for lee-zhur;

Lenth for length;

Len-iant for le-niant;

Le-*pan*-to for *lep*-an-to;

*Lep*er for *lep*-er;

Leth-ar-gic for le-*thar*-gic;

Lev-er for *lever*;

(Licorice) *lic*-er-ish for *lic*-or-is;

La-loc for *li*lac;

Livelong for livelong;

(Loath) lŏth for lŏth;

*Ly*ceum for ly-*ce*-um;

Mam*mil*lary for *mam*mil-lary;

Ma-nor for *man*or;

(Mansuetude) man-*su*-e-tood for *man*-swe-tude;

Man-tu-a-maker for *man*-tu-maker;

Ma-ry-gold for *mar*-ygold;

Markit for market;

Masculine for *masculin*;

Mat-ron for *mā*-tron;

Mātronage for mat-ronage;

Mat-ron-ly for mā-tron-ly;

Mattrass for *mattress*;

(Measure) mā-zhur for *mezh-ur*;

(Medicine) *medsn* for *medesin*;

(Meerschaum) *mere-shawm* for *mairshowm*;

Mellah for mellow;

(Menagery) menajery for me*nah*zhery;

Meni*ng*itis for menin*ji*-tis;

Me*tal*lurgy for metal-*urgy*;

*Mi*croscope for *micro*-scope;

Microscopy for micros-copy;

Meracle for mir-acle;

Mischevas for mis-chie-vous;

Mis-chuf for mis-chief;

Mois-ten for moisn.

Monaco for Mon-a-co;

Mo-nolog for monologue;

(Morphine) morpheen for morfin;

Morsl for morsel;

(Mountain) mounting or mountaine for mount-in;

Museum for mu-ze-um;

(Myrmedon) mur-me-don for meer-me-don;

My-thology for myth-ology;

Necked for na-ked;

Nap for nape;

Nasent for nas-cent;

(National) na-shun-al for nash-un-al;

(Nausea) naw-see-a for naw-she-a;

(Ne'er) nère for nair;

(Nicotine) nic-o-teen for nic-o-tin;

(None) nöne for nun;

Obdurate for ob-durate;

O-be-sity for ob-es-ity;

Ob-sce-nity for ob-scen-ity;

(Official) o-fish-al for of-fishal;

Oft-en for ofn;

Old-en for oldn;

Om-brellar for umbrella;

Onerous for on-er-ous;

Op-ponent for op-po-nent;

Or-inj for or-ange;

Or-de-al for or-de-al;

(Orifice) o-ri-fis for or-i-fis;

(Original) orig-o-nal for o-rij-i-nal;

Overt for o-vert;

(Oxide) ox-eyed for ox-id;

Pa-me-la for Pam-ela;

Pantomine for pan-to-mime;

Pap-yrus for pa-py-rus;

(Paraffine) parafeen for para-fin;

Parsl for par-cel;

Pa-ri-ah for Par-iah;

*Part*sipl for *par*-ti-ci-ple ;
Pa-ta-tah for po-*ta*-to ;
*Patt*ridge for *partridge* ;
Path-os for *pa*-thos ;
Pat-riot for *pa*-triot ;
(Pedagogue) pedagŏg for *ped*-a-gog ;
(Pedagogy) *ped*agoggy for *ped*a-go-jy ;
Pedestal for *ped*-es-tal ;
Pegasus for *Peg*asus ;
Pensl for *pen*cil ;
Piny for *pe*-o-ny ;
Per-ul for peril ;
Persia (*Perzhia*) for Per-shia ;
Pha-ton for pha-e-ton ;
(Pharmaceutic) pharma-kutic for phar-ma-*su*-tic ;
(Pharmacopœia) phar-macopea for pharma-co-*pe*-a ;
Phys-i-*on*-omy for phys-i-*og*-no-my ;
(Pianist) *pee*-a-nist for pee-*ah*-nist ;
(Pigeon) *pij*-*in* for *pij*-*on* ;
Pinchers for *pin*-cers ;

(Piquant) pi*kant* for *pik*-ant ;
Plac-a-ble for *pla*-ca-ble ;
Pla-*ti*-num for *plat*-i-num ;
Ple-bee-an for ple-*be*-ian ;
Ple*thor*a for *pleth*-o-ra ;
Poe*taste*-er for poet-*as*-ter ;
Po-lice for po-*lice* ;
Polliwog for polliwig ;
(Pompeii) Pompey-eye for Pomp*a*-ye ;
Pot-able for pŏ-table ;
Pot-entate for *po*-tentate ;
Pre-bend for *preb*-end ;
Pres-e-dence for pre-*ce*-dence ;
Pré-cize-ly for pre-cise-ly ;
Pred-i-lec-tion for pre-di-lec-tion ;
Pre-*fer*-able for *pref*-er-a-ble ;
Pre-late for *prel*-ate ;
Prem-at-toor for pre-ma-ture ;
Pre-sage for *pres*-age ;
(Prescient) présh-ent for pre-she-ent ;

(Presentation) pre-zenta-tion for *prez*-entation;

Pre-zent-iment for pre-*sent*-iment;

(Presumptuous) *pre-zum-shus* for pre-*zump*-tu-ous;

*Pret*ense for pre*tense*;

*Pret*ty for *pritty*;

•Pre*vent*-a-tive for pre-*vent*-ive;

Pris*tine* for *pris*tin;

Priv-a-cy for *pri*-va-cy;

Pro-bi-ty for *prob*-ity;

(Process) pro̅-cess for *pros-ess*;

Pro-duce for prod-uce;

Pro-duct for *prod*-uct;

Pro-gress for *prog*-ress;

Pro-ject-ile for pro-ject-il;

Prom-ul-gate for pro-*mul*-gate;

Pro-*scen*-i-um for pro-*sce*-nium;

Pro-testation for prot-est-ation;

Pro-tho-*no*-ta-ry for pro-*thon*-a-ta-ry;

Pu-er-*ile* for pu-er-il;

*Pun*kin for pump-kin;

Pur*port* for *pur*port;

Pyri*medal* for pyr*am*-i-dal;

(Pyrites) *py-rites* for pi-*ri*-tes;

Py-ro-technic for pyr-o-tek-nic;

Py-tho-ness for pyth-o-ness;

(Quay) kay or quay for kee;

Quog-mire for quäg-mire;

(Quoit) *kwate* for *qwoit*;

Red-ish for *rad*-ish;

(Rapine) rapeen for *rap*-in;

(Raspberry) *roz*-berry for raz-berry;

Ruther for rather;

(Ration) rash-un for ra-shon;

(Rational) *rash*onal for *rash*-on-al;

Re-ly for *re*-ally;

Rebl for reb-el;

Re-ciprocity for *rec*-i-procity;

Rec-on-ize for *rec*-og-nize;

Re-collect for *rec*-ollect;

Re-con-noitre for *rec*-on-noitre;

Re-kud for *record*;

Re-creant for *rec*-reant;

Re*flu*ent for *ref*-lu-ent;

Re-*med*-iable for reme-diable;

Re*par*-able for *rep*-a-ra-ble;

*Rep*tile for *rep*-til;

Re*pu*table for *rep*-utable;

Res-piratory for res*pi*-ra-tory;

Re-*vo*-cable for *rev*-o-ca-ble;

Rumatiz for rheu-ma-tism;

(Rhubarb) rubub for *rhoo*-barb;

Re-bald for *rib*-ald;

Resk for risk;

*Ro*bust for ro*bust*;

Ro-mo-la for *Rom*-o-la;

Ro-se-*o*-la for ro-*ze*-ola;

(Rothschild) Roth-child for Rote-sheeld;

(Route) *rowt* for *rōōt*;

Sa-cer-do-tal for *sas*-er-dotal;

Sa-cra-ment for *sac*-ra-ment;

Sa-cri-fice for *sac*-rifice;

Sa-cri-lij-us for sac-ri-le-gious;

Sa-gash-us for sa-*ga*-cious;

(Said) sâde for sed;

Sal-ic for Sa-lic;

Sa-leen for sa-line;

Sav-er for sal-ver;

Sanguine for sangwin;

Sar*donyx* for *sar*-do-nyx;

*Sass*aparilla for sar-sa-pa-*ri*lla;

Satisfised for satisfied;

*Sa*turnine for sat-ur-nine;

Sassy for sau-cy;

Sek-a-tary for *secretary*;

Sickl pear for *seck*-el pear;

(Seneschal) sen-es-cal for *sen*eshal;

Senil for *se*-nile;

Short-livd for short-*lived*;

Sreek for shriek;

Srill for shrill;

Srink for shrink;

Srug for shrug;

Si-mo-ny for sim-ony;

Sence for since;

Sin-ecure for *si*-ne-cure;

Slick for sleek;

(Sobriquet) *soobriket* or sou-bri-kā for *sŏ*-bri-kā;

Soft-en for *sofn*;

Sŏ-le-cism for sol-e-cism;

Spazum for spasm;

(Specialty) spesh-i-*al*-i-ty for *spesh*-ialty;

Stomp for stamp;

Stent for stint;

*Stol*id for *stol*-id;

Strenth for strength;

(Suavity) soo-av-ity for swav-ity;

*Sub*jected for sub-*ject*ed;

Sech for such;

Sud'n for sudden;

(Suite) soot for swēēt;

Soopl for *supp*le;

Spose for sup-*pose*;

Sup-prise for sur-prise;

Sword for sŏrd;

Tab-er-*nac*-cle for *tab*-er-nacle;

Tar-tarean for Tar*tā*-rean;

To͠ssl for tassel;

Tatter-de-*ma*-lion f o r tatterde*mal*-ion;

Tah-vern for *tav*ern;

Tit for teat;

Tele*graph*er for tel*eg*-rapher;

Tele*graphy* for tel*egra*-phy;

*Te*nable for *ten*able;

Tenet for *ten*et;

Tepid for *tep*id;

(Terpsichore) *Terpsi*-core for Terp-*sic*-or-e;

Tha-lia for Tha-*li*-a;

Thyme for *tyme*;

*Tick*elish for ticklish;

Tin-y for ti-ny;

*Tol*stoï for Tol-*sto*-ee;

To-po-graphic for top-ographic;

Tor-toise for *tortis*;

(Turgenief or Tourgue-nieff) *Tur*-ge-nef for Toor-*gain*-yef;

To*ward* for *to*ward (tŏrd);

Travl for *travel*;

Tremendyus for tremen-dous;

Tri-bune for *trib*-une;

(Troche) trochy for *tro-kee*;

Toon for tune;

Tyr-an-nic for ty-ran-nic;

Ty-ran-ny for tyr-anny;

Unk-shus for unc-tu-ous;

Uni*vo*cal for u*niv*-o-cal;

Un-*pre*-ce-dented for un-*prec*-edented;

Va-ga-ry for va*ga*ry;

Valuble for *val*-u-a-ble;

*Vari*acose for *varicose*;

Var-i-loid for var-ioloid;

Vaws for vāse;

Ve-*hem*ence for *ve*-he-mence;

Ve-*he*-ment for *ve*-he-ment;

Velvit for velvet;

*Vet*rinary for vet-er-in-ary;

Vide*li*cet for vide*li*cet;

(Villain) villun for *vilin*;

V*in*dicatory for *vin*-dica-tory;

(Violoncello) violin-cello for vee-o-lon-*chel*-lo;

*Vi*rago for virago;

Vis-count for *vi*-count;

(Visor) *vi*-zor for *viz*-or;

Voc-a-ble for *vo*-cable;

Vol-a-tile for *volatil*;

Wagner for *Vahg-ner*;

(Weapon) wĕp'n for *wep'n*;

Worf for wharf;

Wich for which;

Windah for window;

Wisky for whiskey;

Windurd for windward;

(Women) wimun for *wim-en*;

Wunt for wŏn't;

Wuth for worth;

(Wrestle) rassl for res'l;

(Yacht) *yat* for *yot*;

Yit for yet;

Zo-di-*ac*-al for zo-*di*-acal;

Zoo-ological for zō-ologi-cal.

CHAPTER XVI.

TERMS MISAPPLIED.

Mrs. Malaprop, Mrs. Partington, and the Duc de Beaufort are conspicuous examples of persons using inappropriate or wrong words to express their ideas. But we see frequently not only in the hasty work of newspaper writers, but even in the productions of famous authors, mistakes that should have been avoided. Many words, judged by their derivation, are used incorrectly in common speech, but have so long passed current that, like coins re-stamped, it is idle to object to their use. Examples of some of the more popular mistakes in the use of words here follow :

Ability for capacity. Capacity in comprehension; ability in execution.

Above for more than or beyond. The river is *above* fifty yards wide. The task was *above* his strength.

Administer for deal. A blow administered.

Aggravate for exasperate, provoke, irritate. His conduct *aggravated* me.

Against for when. Have it ready *against* I come.

Aggregate for amount to. The collection *aggregated* $500. The two purses given the minister *aggregated* $1,000. Aggregate is a transitive verb.

Ain't for isn't. *Ain't* it nice !

All not for not all. *All* the members were *not* present.

Allow for think, opine, or claim. He *allows* he has the right on his side.

Alternation for succession. An alternation of suitors.

Alternative for course. He had three *alternatives* left.

Amount for degree. He has attained a remarkable amount of perfection [degree of excellence].

Antagonize for oppose. He *antagonized* the Dean's views.

Any for at all. I am not reading *any* now. She does not hear *any*.

Appreciate for value or esteem. I *appreciate* him highly.

Approach for address, appeal to. The party *approached* the Park Commissioner.

Apt for likely or liable. He is *apt* to be fishing. If you speak you will be *apt* to cause trouble.

As for that. I don't know *as* I shall.

As for so (after a negative). John is not *as* good
·   as William.

Aside for apart. *Aside* from this consideration.

As though for as if. It seems *as though* he were crazy. [This use of though is as old as Chaucer, who, in speaking of the miller, says :

" *His berd as ony sowe or fox was reed
And therto brood* as though *it were a spade.*"

The translators of the Bible made use of it. It
is to be found in nearly every writer of English,
and in poetry is certainly justifiable. Yet in
ordinary writing *as if* is preferable.]

At for by. The house was sold *at* auction.

Avocation for vocation. His *avocation* prevents
him from going into society. [Etymologically
the distinction between these two words justifies their separation; it gives a useful term of
contract between one's duties and one's diver-
sions.]

Badly for very much. I shall miss you *badly*.

Balance for rest or remainder. He sold the *balance*
of the edition.

Be done with for have done with. He said he soon
would be done with it.

Beat for defeat. We beat the enemy.

Before for rather than. He chooses death *before*
disgrace.

Benedict for Benedick. The young man has recently become a *Benedict*. [Benedick, as a
byword for a newly married man, comes from
Benedick, the young gentleman in "Much Ado
About Nothing," who ridicules love and finally
marries Beatrice. A Benedict is either one of
the fourteen popes of this name, or else a
monk of the order of the Benedictines. For a
bachelor the name "Benedict" is, however,

allowable, as it is probably not the result of a confusion with the name of Shakespeare's hero, but an allusion to the celibacy of the Benedictine sect.]

Between for among. *Between* us three. [Between is used only of two; among of more than two.]

Better for more than. He received *better* than five dollars.

Bi-weekly for semi-weekly. A *bi-weekly* steamer sailing every other Saturday. [Bi-weekly means twice a week.]

Blame it on for charge or accuse. He *blamed* it *on* me.

Bogus for worthless or fraudulent. A *bogus* coin.

Both alike for alike. They *both* look *alike.*

Bound for doomed, destined, or determined. It is *bound* to fail. I am *bound* to win.

But for only or that. The others *but* gave a cent.

But for only or that or than. I don't doubt *but* he will come. No other excuse *but* this was given.

Cablegram for cable despatch. A *cablegram* from London.

Calculate for purpose, intend. I *calculate* to go to Europe this summer.

Calligraphy for chirography. His *calligraphy* is illegible.

Can for may. *Can* I have some more strawberries?

Capacious for large. There was a *capacious* rent in the bottom of the ship.

Centrifugal for tangential. [When a wet mop is

spun round to dry it, the water does not fly from the centre, that is, centrifugally, but from the edge, and at right angles to a line drawn from the centre; that is, at a tangent, or sideways. You can simulate this fact by whirling a stick round and round and suddenly letting it go, — not throwing it, — when it will fly away, not in a straight line from the shoulder, but sideways. The waves made by dropping a stone into a pond, the light from the sun, and sound and heat are examples of centrifugal force.]

Claim for assert, maintain. He claimed that he had lost his pocketbook.

Clever for good-natured. He is a *clever* fellow.

Condign for severe. He deserves *condign* [that is, deserved] punishment.

Contemptible for contemptuous. I hold a *contemptible* opinion of him.

Creditably for credibly. He is *creditably* informed of the thing.

Cyclone for tornado or hurricane. A terrible *cyclone* struck the ship.

Denude for exhausted. The lake was *denuded* of its fish.

Deputize for depute. He was *deputized* to go to the king.

Description for kind. He had no furs of any description.

Deteriorate from for detract from. " Does it in

your eyes deteriorate from Milton's peculiar greatness that he could not have given us the conception of Falstaff?" (Dean Farrar.)

Develops for turns out, becomes known. It develops that six men were engaged in the conspiracy.

Different to for different from. It is different to what it used to be.

Directly for when or as soon as. *Directly* he came in he began his work.

Dirt for earth or loam. They built a *dirt* road.

Disposition for disposal. What *disposition* shall I make of the MS.?

Disremember for forget. I disremember when it took place.

Dock for wharf. He fell off the *dock*.

Don't for doesn't. He don't do it.

Drank for drunk. I have *drank* the medicine.

Each other for one another (of more than two). The three women kissed *each other*.

Elegant for beautiful. This is an elegant morning.

Endorse for approve. I *endorse* this sentiment.

Enthuse for to grow or make enthusiastic. Her rendition of the song *enthused* him! I was real enthused!

Epithet for term of abuse or byword. We are told, in a recent text-book on physiography, that certain islands " have been called the ' Brooches of the Sea,' and well deserve the *epithet* from their attractiveness." [Instead of epithet, of course, metaphor should have been used.] All adjectives, whether opprobrious or complimentary are epithets; also nouns used as adjectives, or having the descriptive functions of adjectives, such as titles of honor, are epithets; *e.g.*, Lord Wolseley, Sir John, Cardinal Newman, William the Conqueror, *Pater Æneas*, Washington, *the father of his country*. Such terms as fool, liar, brute, are not epithets, but their adjectives, foolish, lying, brutal, are. An epithet does not necessarily mean anything abusive; the words beautiful, homely, truthful, pious, are epithets.

Equally as well for equally well. His autograph would do *equally as well*.

Every for all possible. We have taken *every pains*, and extended him *every* courtesy.

Every now and then for now and then. He comes to see us *every* now and then.

Expect for suppose. I *expect* you were *sick* yesterday.

Extend for show.

Female for woman. [This use of *female* was common in fiction a few years ago, but better taste discards it.]

Final completion for completion. On its *final* completion the store will be used by its builders.

Find for provide. The pupils will *find* their own books.

Fix for arrange, repair, etc. He *fixed* her hair. The clock stopped, but I *fixed* it. He *fixed up*

and went. [Fix has been called "the American
word of words." It is a word of all work.
Good taste would suggest discrimination and
variety in the choice of verbs. Fix means to
establish.]

Fly for flee. The enemy was seen to *fly*. [That
would be correct if it referred to Harpies.]

Folks for folk. My folks are well. [This plural of
folk, which is itself plural, has become so common as to be almost justified.]

For the future for thereafter or afterwards. They
resided in the city *for the future*.

Fraud for impostor. The court proved to be a
fraud.

Future for subsequent. His *future* career is unknown.

Gents for gentlemen. *Gents* wear *pants*. [When
possible it is better to say men than gentlemen.]

Goods for material. She had a dress made out of
excellent goods.

Gums for rubbers. It is raining; wear your gums.
[Some purists object also to the use of the
word rubbers, and would insist on using the
word rubber-shoes or over-shoes.]

Had ought for ought. He *had ought* to go.

Hain't for have not. I *hain't got* it.

Handicapped for hampered or hindered. He was
badly handicapped by his accident.

Handy for near by. The post-office is handy to the
house.

Have [has] got for have [has]. He has got a bicycle.

Healthy for wholesome. Oranges are *healthy* eating. [We may speak of *healthy* surroundings,
wholesome advice, *healthful* occupations.]

Het for heated. The room was *het* by a stove.

However for how. *However* could you do so?

Home for at home. Is your mother home?

Hung for hanged; of persons. The defaulter
hung himself.

Hurry up for make haste. He told her to *hurry
up* and come down.

Idea for opinion. It is my *idea* that it will rain
to-morrow.

If for whether. I doubt if the letter ever reached
him.

In for into. He threw the boy *in* the water. He
went *in* the house.

In evidence for prominent, or conspicuous, or even
present. At Mrs. Jones' Count Gold-hunter
was *in evidence*.

In respect of for with respect to. We have considered the matter *in* respect *of* which we were
talking.

Inaugurate for begin or open. The exercises were
inaugurated with music by the band.

[Indices is not the proper English plural of index
in the sense of a table of contents. The Latin
plural indices applies to mathematical signs,
and to the medical equivalent to critical days.

It is better to preserve a similar distinction also
with the two plurals of appendix.]

Individual for person. There were six distin-
guished individuals present.

Inside of for within; of time. He will be here
inside of two weeks.

Kids for gloves or children. She told the *kids* to
put on their kids!

Kind of a for kind of. What kind of a speech did
he make?

Know as for know that. I don't know as I can.

Last for latter (of two). There are two houses on
that side. You want to go to the *last* one.

Latter for last (of more than two). There were
six books in a row. I took the latter.

Lay for lie. There let him *lay*. [Lay is a transitive verb. A hen lays eggs. A mason lays
bricks. The preterit is laid: The hen laid
eggs. I laid the book on the table. Lie is
intransitive. I lie on the ground. The preterit
is lay: I lay on the ground. I laid my cloak
down and lay on it.]

Learn for teach. He *learned* me to draw.

Leave for let or allow. Leave go! *Leave alone of* it!

Less for fewer. There were not *less* than ten appli-
cants.

Liable for likely. He is liable to break his leg.

Like for as. He speaks *like* I do. [Like requires
an object only. As requires a verb expressed
or understood. It is as yellow as gold]

Like for, as if. It looks *like* it would snow.

Lit for lighted. The gas was *lit* at six o'clock.

Loan for lend. I will *loan* you a book.

Locate for settle. He *located* near Seattle.

Lots for many or much. We have *lots* of apples this year, and *lots* of trouble in gathering them.

Lunch for luncheon. Gents who wear pants eat *lunch*.

Lurid for bright or red. The sky was *lit* with a lurid glow. When he came in he gave us a lurid description of the fire. [Lurid means pale or gloomy.]

Majority for most. The *majority* of the bonds were sold at par.

Materialize for appear. We expected them Sunday, but they did not *materialize*.

Mind for obey. Boys should *mind* their parents.

Monogram for monograph. He wrote a *monogram* on church music.

Most for almost or nearly. I see him *most* every day.

Mutual for common. Mutual enmities cement friendships. [This use of mutual for common, called by Macaulay a vulgarism, has its justification in a genuine need in the language. Nevertheless, as in the example given, it often introduces a wrong concept, and should be used sparingly. There can be no misconstruction of the epithet mutual in " Our Mutual Friend," for instance ; it sounds better than our common friend, and is not open to the possible secondary meaning of common.]

Name for mention. I never *named* the affair to him.

Neither, or, for neither, nor. *Neither* John or I *were* present. [There seems to be a conflict of authority regarding the use of the alternatives. Thus the Standard Dictionary upholds the use of *nor* after *not*. But it seems like piling up double negatives to say, Not John nor William nor Thomas. The *not* governs the whole, and one should say, Not John or William or Thomas. On the other hand, it is correct to say, John did not speak, nor did I. So, also, after *never*. I never saw Shakespeare or Milton, is correct, when *nor* would be wrong.]

Nicely for *well*. I am *nicely* to-day.

No use for of no use. It is *no use* complaining. [Better, It is of no use to complain.]

Nothing like as for not nearly so. Cuba is *nothing like as* pleasant as Hawaii.

On for by or in. The book is sold on subscription. I came on the cars. [The English prefer *in the street* to *on the street*. But owing to the distinction between on the street and on the sidewalk, the American locution will undoubtedly prevail. It is certainly logical and defensible. When a man says he lives " in Fifth Avenue " he seems to imply an out-of-door existence not conveyed by the term " on Fifth Avenue."]

Only for except. The *electrics* will not stop only at the white posts. [Only is the sworn enemy of accuracy and elegance. It should be placed next the word or phrase that it modifies. Thus Mr. Aldrich, in his poem, writes, "I *only* died last night." But surely, it may be argued, language is not so formal and ironclad that a poet must turn his poetry into prose in order to be precise. Not at all! And all that one would wish is that a writer or speaker should not sacrifice sense to slipshod haste. If the meaning is plain, euphony is preferable to preciseness, as in the sentence, "He only lived for their sakes." There seems to be a similar fatality about misplacement attaching to the words also, chiefly, scarcely. A little thought will lead one to an instinctive sense of the proper place for these adverbs.]

Overflown for overflowed. The pond has *overflown* its shores.

Own for confess. I *own* I was wrong.

Pants for trousers or breeches. There is less excuse for this vulgar contraction than there is for gents, which has indeed good old English authority.

Party for person. Are you the *party* I met last night?

Patronage for custom. John Johnson, successor to John Smith, solicits your patronage.

Per for a. This tea is sold for $1.00 *per* pound.

Three dollars *per* volume. [Per should be used only before Latin words: per annum, per centum, etc.]

Perpetually for continually. Careless writers *perpetually* misuse will for shall. [There is a distinction worth preserving in the use of the words constant, continual, continuous, perpetual, and their adverbs. The careless writer that uses one word for another may not make the mistake frequently, but misuses it whenever the chance occurs: he *constantly* misuses will for shall. Sometimes by accident the careless writer may use the word correctly: he *continually* uses will for shall. Perpetually gives an exaggerated concept. It means more than incessant. The perpetual flow of a river: the incessant may cease; the perpetual continues for ever!]

Perspicuity for perspicacity. He is a man of great *perspicuity*. [Perspicuity means clearness. Perspicacity means clear-sighted, keen. Perspicuity is objective, perspicacity subjective. A person of perspicacity expresses himself with perspicuity.]

Pianiste for pianist. The pianiste performed her solo handsomely. [Pianist is English; pianiste is French; both are used without change of sex termination.]

Plead for pleaded. He *plead* his cause. He has *plead* his cause. [Here pleaded should be used in both cases.]

Portion for part. In what *portion* of the country do you *reside?* [It is, however, correct to ask at a hotel to be served a single portion.]

Posted for informed. He is well posted as to his duties.

Predicate for predict. It is impossible to *predicate* what he will do. On the other hand, predict is sometimes used for predicate.

Presumptive for presumptuous. He was exceedingly presumptive in his demands.

Preventative for preventive. Quinine is a *preventative* for chills and fever. [The rule, in the formation of adjectives from nouns ending in *ation*, is to add *ative*, *e.g.*, communication — communicative; representation — representative; and from nouns ending in *ion* to add *tive*, *e.g.*, deception — deceptive; prevention — preventive.]

Previous for previously. Previous to his coming I saw him.

Privilege for right. Our *privilege* is universal suffrage. [A privilege is a special or peculiar right, or not a right at all.]

Propose for purpose. I *propose* to go to the theatre this evening.

Proven for proved. It was *proven* that he was a forger.

Quite for rather. It is *quite* a warm day. [Quite means fully, completely.] Is the gentleman quite done? [It is colloquial to use it with the indefinite article to mean considerable, or with an article to mean a little. Nevertheless, out of colloquialisms grows racy idiomatic English. And such phrases as " He cuts quite a dash " atone by their vigor for lack of elegance.]

Raise for rear. She *raised* three children. [Had this term been applied to pigs it would be correct. It is also incorrect to speak of raising rent.]

Rarely for very. It was a *rarely* beautiful evening. [It is a moot point whether to use rarely or rare in such a sentence as : It is rarely that one hears of such an accident. Rarely means infrequently, and although it is better to say " One rarely hears," the pariphrasis may be defended.]

Rarely ever for rarely if ever. I *rarely ever* see him.

Real for very. Ain't she real cute? [Those who use this vulgarism are apt to pronounce it as if it were spelt *reel.*]

Rendition for rendering or performance. Patti gave a superb *rendition* of her *encore !* [Rendition is properly applied to the yielding up of a fortress or the trying of lard.]

Replace for displace. The school committee replaced the algebra *by* geometry. [Often also replace is used where take the place or places of would be better. The great orators have gone : who will replace them ?]

Retire for withdrawn or draw out. The government has begun to retire the paper currency. [Some persons wishing to be overnice speak of retiring instead of going to bed.]

Rugged for sturdy, robust. He is a rugged boy.

Ruination for ruin. It will be the *ruination* of him.

Run for manage. Who *runs* his business for him?

Sabbath for Sunday. I will come next *Sabbath*.

Seldom ever for seldom if ever, or seldom or never. We *seldom ever* meet. Seldom or ever is meaningless.

Set for sit. Is the hen *setting?* Take a seat and *set* down. [One sets the hen; but the hen sits on the eggs.]

Settle for pay. When did he *settle* his bill?

Simply for absolutely. The concert was simply delicious.

Since for ago. I came a week since. Since when is tautological. My tire was punctured; since when I have not ridden. Since when did he fail?

Smart for fashionable. A number of the smart set are sailing next month.

Some for somewhat. It rained some. I think some of buying a seashore residence.

Some place for somewhere. I have lost my purse. I must have left it some place.

State for say. He stated that he was forty-six. [State means to set out the particulars in detail.]

Stop for stay. At what hotel are you *stopping?* [To stop means to cease.]

Subsequent for subsequently. The peace was made subsequent to their defeat.

Supposititious for imaginary, hypothetical. In the *supposititious* event of his coming, you will cause his arrest. [Supposititious means counterfeit; but its look and sound connect it in the common mind with *suppose*.]

Sustain for receive. He sustained an injury to his knee.

Than for when. Scarcely had I spoken *than* the door opened.

These kind for this kind. *These kind* of blows kill.

Those kind for that kind. *Those kind* of pears are delicious. [It must be confessed that this colloquialism is ingrained in the common English speech, preserved in literature as it is in the works of Bacon and many others.]

To for at. I was to church this morning. [Nevertheless, in spite of the rule, since the verb to be is sometimes used idiomatically for to go, the expression I have been to church, I have been to the theatre this afternoon, may possibly be defended.]

Towards for toward. The shots flew towards six soldiers. [Anything that shall reduce the sibilance of our English tongue is welcome. The final *s* on all words compounded with *ward* is superfluous.]

Transferrence for transfer. I attended to the *transferrence* of the bonds.

Transpire for occur, take place, happen, or elapse. The great Boston fire *transpired* in 1872; twenty years have *transpired* since then. [Transpire means to leak out, become known. It transpired that his father was a forger.]

Try for make. He will *try* the experiment this afternoon.

Unbeknownst for unknown. She came in unbeknownst to me.

Under weigh for under way. We got *under weigh* at sunrise. [To weigh means to lift, as to weigh anchor, but way, nautically speaking, indicates motion or progress through the water.]

Usage for use. The *usage* of the split infinitive seems to be on the increase.

Venal for venial. He was guilty of a venal sin. [Venal means ready to be bought, mercenary. Venial corresponds to pardonable.]

Vulgar for immodest, obscene. Do not listen to *vulgar* stories. [Vulgar properly means low, coarse, and ill-bred.]

Ways for way. He came a long *ways* with me.

What for that. I do not doubt *but what* I shall see him there. [In the locution, He brought in nothing but what he paid duty on, it is correctly used.]

Who for whom. Who did you see? [It may be fairly argued that this is a condensed form for, Who is it that you saw? This objective use of who belongs in the same category as, It is me, It is him. Nice writers will not fall into this colloquialism. Yet those that enjoy idiomatic speech will not hesitate to use it in common conversation.]

Whom for who. We saw the explorer *whom* they said was the bravest man living.

Will for shall. We *will* move, on the first of January, to our new store. [*Will* in the first person, singular and plural, denotes a promise, expresses will. Shall denotes future action. Will I bring my violin ? asks the careless musician. How can his hostess know what he will do ? Shall I bring my violin? would imply that permission was sought.]

Without for unless. He will not go on the stage *without* his father consents.

Worst for worse. If *worst* comes to worst.

Worst kind for exceedingly. I want to see her *worst kind !*

Would for should. We would not shed a tear if the man was hanged. [The truth is, failure to discriminate in the proper use of these auxiliaries deprives our language of its inheritance of niceness and accuracy. But it is often difficult to decide on the proper word to use, particularly when the sentence is complicated by indirect discourse. The New York " Evening Sun," in the sentence " They feel confident that out of the 3,500 men they *will* be able to call talent that

shall send the department ahead," manages to misuse both auxiliaries. The Frenchman said: " I *will* drown; no one *shall* help me ! "]
You was for you were. *Was you* there?

Mistakes in Comparison. — We often make mistakes in comparisons of adjectives by omitting the exclusive " other " with comparatives and inserting it with superlatives.

St. Peter's is larger than any church in the world. That would imply that it was larger than itself or that it was not a church.

The London " Times " alleged that Mr. Stanley was the only one of his predecessors who slaughtered the natives of the region he passed through.

They were the most audacious of all the *other* enemies.

Where two objects are compared it is a mistake to use the superlative degree. John was the *tallest* of my two sons. In the same way the poem errs when it says: " And lo! Ben Adhem's name led all the rest."

Mistakes in Use of Pronouns. — Careless writers fail to discriminate in the use and position of pronouns. Much confusion often arises from the lack in English of distinctive pronouns like the French *celui-ci, celui-là.* Thus of two or three men: He told him that if he did not pay him within a week he would cause him to turn over to him the property that he had just bought of him.

The possibilities of misunderstanding that sentence are multiplied. So of *she* and *her*. It requires great skill to manage these grammatical forms so as to avoid ambiguity.

The misuse of *which* for that is widespread. Few of our most popular modern writers make the distinction, and yet the proper distinction often renders a sentence free from trace of ambiguity.

The rule is simple: *That* should introduce a clause restricting and completing the meaning of the antecedent.

Which and *who* should introduce a new fact concerning the antecedent. I took the only boat *which* I could see. A sentence containing a relative clause with "which" may be ambiguous. A sentence containing a relative clause with "that" properly used cannot be ambiguous. Sometimes the distinction is so unimportant that no one would care to make it, as for instance: The sheep *that* were in the orchard broke loose. The sheep *which* were in the orchard broke loose. In the first instance the sentence implies that the other sheep did not break loose, that there were other sheep. In the second there is no implication that there were other sheep; the sheep broke loose, and the sheep that broke loose were in the pasture.

"You will open the conferences *which* will be held in Paris." Here it is evident that the question of the place to have the conferences is fully decided. They will be held in Paris. Had *that* been used, the order would be plain that there were to be other conferences elsewhere, and that the chancellor was to preside over the ones at Paris. Is not the distinction evident and worth utilizing in other cases ?

In cases where ambiguity might be serious, it is well to use "that" for "who." As for instance: The officers *who* received promotion assembled in the hall. This implies that all the officers received promotion and assembled in the hall.

The officers *that* received promotion assembled in the hall. That implies that only those that received promotion assembled in the hall.

Sometimes careless or ignorant writers misuse "that" for "which."

On the Seine lies the city of Paris, that the Germans occupied in the Franco-Prussian War. That signifies that another city of Paris was not occupied by the Germans.

Professor Compton, in his "Common Errors of Speech," falls into the error that he criticises; he says: "The English language allows a degree of freedom in the use of the passive form *that* is often conducive to rapidity and force, but *which* is, in the present day, much abused."

These distinctions promote precision of language, and should be carefully taught to the young.

It is a mistake to use the reflexive pronouns *myself* for "I," *yourself* for "you," *himself* for "him." John and *myself* came together.

It is a mistake to use pronouns without antecedents, even when the context supplies the missing noun : "The bazaars are interesting centres of observation. Here the potters are engaged in turning their wooden wheels. In Persia they use them as water-coolers." Meaning, of course, the pots made by the potters.

Misplacement of Clauses. — A kindred error is to separate, by a subordinate clause, the pronoun from its antecedent, often giving rise to ludicrous misstatements.

Ludicrous mistakes are often made by the careless introduction of subordinate clauses. "Paid to a woman whose husband was drowned by order of the vestry under London Bridge."

"He was suddenly seized with an attack of paralysis whilst at breakfast, of which he ultimately died."

"Erected to the memory of John Phillips accidentally shot as a mark of affection by his brother."

"He was driving away from the church where he had been married in a coach and four."

A Glasgow paper thus described a shipping accident: "The captain swam ashore, as did also the stewardess. She was insured for £3,000, and carried two hundred tons of pig iron."

Morse's geography tells of a certain town that contains "four hundred houses and four thousand inhabitants, all standing with their gable ends to the street."

An advertisement in the "Times" announced this peculiar need:

"Two sisters want washing."

The following three sacrificed accuracy to economy:

"Shetland pony suitable for a child with a long mane and tail."

"Wanted, a piano by a lady with modern legs."

"Wanted, a nurse for an infant between twenty-five and thirty." — *Telegraph.*

It is often better to break a recalcitrant sentence of this sort into two or even more independent sentences.

A plural noun following a singular will sometimes mislead a writer into using a plural verb. This is called the "error of proximity." "The statement of these facts *were* disagreeable to him." "To Marat, and Danton, and Robespierre *are* due the honor." This is one of the commonest and most insidious of errors. Hundreds of examples might be and have been culled from famous authors.

It is a common error to use a singular verb with the relative following an inclusive superlative:

He is one of the tallest men *who* has ever walked the streets of the metropolis.

Careless writers and speakers often clumsily use the perfect infinitive dependent on a past or perfect verb: I was sorry not *to have seen* you yesterday.

I would have liked to have asked him his name. Here "I should like to have asked" or "I should have liked to ask " are the proper forms, there being a slight difference in meaning between the two.

He declared that he should have been proved to have spoken those words.

Here there is ambiguity; because *he* might refer to the one that declared or to another person ; *should* might mean *ought to be* or *ought to have been*, and *to have spoken* might or might not stand for the original thought. Verily, indirect discourse in English is beset with difficulties.

Froude is cited as saying : " He might have been expected to have gone." *To go* would be better.

It is a mistake to use the participial construction and neglect the necessary apposition : Having spoken the customary caution, the door was shut. Miss Austen, in " Pride and Prejudice," wrote : " Amazed at the alteration in her manner, every sentence that he uttered increased her embarrassment."

An " Old Soldier" justifies the title of his book (" Rough Notes ") by this sentence : " Being early killed, I sent a party in search of his mangled body."

Carelessness in the Use of Prepositions. — Carelessness in the use of prepositions causes a slovenly style.

Some English writers use *to* for *from*, with the adjective different. He is different *to* his father.

Differ *with* has a different meaning from differ *from*.

Connect to is sometimes used for connect with. A rubber tube connecting to the pump.

Compare to likewise erroneously takes the place of compare with.

He wore a hat ornamented *by* gold galoon.

Sympathize *in* for sympathize with.

Throw in for throw *into.*

Some grammarians animadvert on the use of *between* for " among " where more than two objects are mentioned. In most cases among is certainly preferable. But where the imagination supplies the thought of pairs, between may be justified.

A close union sprang up *between* these four men.

Here among should certainly be used. A constant intercourse prevailed *between* the soldiers of the two opposing armies. Here " between " is defensible.

Some writers use between with every or each. *Between* each musician hung an electric light.

Mrs. Gaskell wrote: " Between every stitch she could look up." A great obstacle interposed between our union. Here the duality of union suggested " between."

It is a mistake to repeat the conjunction that in a sentence where a subordinate clause intervenes between the verb and the dependent clause.

I told him that if he broke the window that he would have to pay for it.

The misplacing of adverbs is a common mistake. *Not only* should be placed so as to qualify the word it affects, and should be followed by *but also.* Few writers are not guilty of carelessly neglecting this simple rule. Thus a literary journal says: Homer was not only the maker of a nation, but of a language and of a religion.

Here either *not only* should follow *maker*, or the words " but also the establisher."

The Split Infinitive. — It is generally a mistake to employ the split or divided infinitive; that is, to separate *to* from its *verb*.

"To in certain measure approve." " I hope to quickly come." Occasionally perfect definiteness seems to require this collocation of the adverb.

" It is said that China hopes to easily procure in France funds to enable her to promptly pay the indemnity."

Here as *easily* might apply to hopes, and as it would awkwardly follow *procure*, " to easily procure," though clumsy, might be pardoned; but the second instance in the same sentence is unpardonable.

"There is a disposition not to tamely yield." Here if *tamely* were placed after *not*, the sentence would be worse and not better. It should read: " Not to yield tamely."

Common-sense and an ear quick to appreciate harmonious combinations should guide in such cases. But the hard and fast rule that would never allow an adverb to separate *to* and its verb is not in accord with the free genius of English. There are so many examples of its infringement by the best and most idiomatic writers of English that no frenzied protest on the part of purists will avail. Yet it is a mistake not to avoid the awkwardness of the split infinitive whenever it is possible to do so.

Never is a word that is frequently misplaced. Ruskin in one sentence says to this effect: "We never remember ever to have seen."

Omission of Articles. — It is a mistake to omit the article when different objects are mentioned under the same régime. He sold the black and white puppies: meaning that he sold the black puppies and the white puppies, and not the puppies of mixed black and white.

The Democratic and Republican parties held their convention. This would imply that it was **a joint** convention.

It is a mistake not to employ the article before the titular adjectives Reverend and Honorable, which are not, like Doctor and Major, titles. The Reverend Doctor Hodgson; the Honorable John Jones; the Venerable Archdeacon Smith. It looks particularly awkward to have the article omitted when the abbreviations are used: "Rev. William Jackson occupied Rev. Mr. Hunt's pulpit." "Hon. Henry Archer was elected to Congress."

By constant study of the best models of English style, by "eternal vigilance" in avoiding ambiguities, by guarding the tongue and the pen, and, above all, the mind, from falling into careless habits one may learn to make this language of ours a beautiful instrument for the expression of thought. One who can write with well-balanced and graceful phrasing, who can speak easily, fluently, and without hesitation and stumbling, and who, above all, has something worth saying, is certain to win the attention of the world.

INDEX.

A brown study under a different color, 204.

Acres and Wiseacres, 208.

Æsop's fables much involved in legend, 96.

Affra capella, translated " African she-goats," 174.

African she-goats, amusing translation of *Affra capella*, 174.

Against the grain, 220.

Agrippina not put to death by Nero, 99.

Ainsworth narrates exploits of Dick Turpin. See Dick Turpin, 168.

À la pipe du jour. See Peep o' Day, 205.

Alexander compared with Thothmes, 90; conquests of, 91; did not weep for other worlds to conquer, 91.

Alfred, King, did not burn the cakes or enact good laws, 119.

" A little more than kin and less than kind," meaning and derivation of, 85.

All is lost save honor, 192.

Aloe, the gardener's fable concerning, 32.

A nation of shopkeepers, originated by Adam Smith, 195.

Anaxarchus, Alexander's favorite philosopher, 91, *note*.

" Ancient Mariner," error of Coleridge in, 171.

Ancient statues were colored and adorned, 59.

A new brougham sweeps clean, 163.

Anglo-Saxons, the, 119.

Anglo-Spanish conflict. See Armada, 145.

Henry II. did not conceal Fair Rosamond, 123.

Hessian boots are not boots worn by Hessians, 218.

Higginson, Francis, declares the Puritans were not separatists, 138.

Hingeston, F. C., translates *Affra capella* "African she-goats," 174.

"History of the Plague." See Defoe, 166.

Hodgkins speaks favorably of Nero, 99.

"Hog" used in Yorkshire for a sheep a year old, 195, *note*.

Holiday, no national, 72; legal, in the various States, 72–75.

Holland, doubtful derivation of name, 19.

Hollyhocks a sort of hoax, 33.

Holmes, Oliver Wendell, on the nautilus, 54.

Homout Ich Dene signed by the Black Prince, 127.

Horatius and the bridge, story of, 94.

House-fly, the, formation of feet of, 52.

How a bull charges, 37.

How deep-sea fish fall up, 57.

Hudson's Bay should be called a sea, 21.

Hugo, Victor, mathematical blunder of, 172; misspells English proper names, 172; on Cambronne's words at Waterloo, 189.

Hurricane, definition of, 89.

Huss did not say "Sancta simplicitas," or pun on his own name, 191.

Ibis, the scarlet, not the sacred ibis, 49.

Ice in Iceland, 14.

In the soup, 220; a *purée* soup not a pure soup, 220.

"Irish apricots." See Rabbits and Rarebits, 208.

Irish, origin of the, 96.

Iron Duke, the name derived from an iron steamship, 180.

Iron mask, story of the, 158.

Irving, Washington, and the monks of Newstead, 155.